CANADA IN QUESTION

Exploring Our Citizenship in the Twenty-First Century

(in) UTP insights

UTP Insights is an innovative collection of brief books offering accessible introductions to the ideas that shape our world. Each volume in the series focuses on a contemporary issue, offering a fresh perspective anchored in scholarship. Spanning a broad range of disciplines in the social sciences and humanities, the books in the UTP Insights series contribute to public discourse and debate and provide a valuable resource for instructors and students.

For a list of books published in the series, see page 121.

CANADA IN QUESTION

Exploring Our Citizenship
in the Twenty-First Century

Peter MacKinnon

UNIVERSITY OF TORONTO PRESS
Toronto Buffalo London

© University of Toronto Press 2022
Toronto Buffalo London
utorontopress.com
Printed in Canada

ISBN 978-1-4875-4313-6 (cloth)   ISBN 978-1-4875-4315-0 (EPUB)
ISBN 978-1-4875-4314-3 (paper)   ISBN 978-1-4875-4316-7 (PDF)

Library and Archives Canada Cataloguing in Publication

Title: Canada in question : exploring our citizenship in the twenty-first
   century / Peter MacKinnon.
Names: MacKinnon, Peter, author.
Series: UTP insights.
Description: Series statement: UTP insights | Includes bibliographical
   references and index.
Identifiers: Canadiana (print) 20210335556 | Canadiana (ebook)
   20210335602 | ISBN 9781487543136 (cloth) | ISBN 9781487543143
   (paper) | ISBN 9781487543150 (EPUB) | ISBN 9781487543167 (PDF)
Subjects: LCSH: Citizenship – Canada.
Classification: LCC JL187 .M33 2022 | DDC 323.60971 – dc23

We wish to acknowledge the land on which the University of Toronto
Press operates. This land is the traditional territory of the Wendat, the
Anishnaabeg, the Haudenosaunee, the Métis, and the Mississaugas of the
Credit First Nation.

University of Toronto Press acknowledges the financial support of the
Government of Canada, the Canada Council for the Arts, and the Ontario Arts
Council, an agency of the Government of Ontario, for its publishing activities.

**Canada Council   Conseil des Arts
for the Arts   du Canada**

ONTARIO ARTS COUNCIL
CONSEIL DES ARTS DE L'ONTARIO
an Ontario government agency
un organisme du gouvernement de l'Ontario

Funded by the   Financé par le
Government   gouvernement
of Canada   du Canada

Canada

MIX
Paper from
responsible sources
FSC   FSC® C016245

For Canada and Canadians

Contents

Preface

In paying public tribute to soldiers fallen early in the Peloponnesian War, and to the city that was their home, Greek orator Pericles remarked that Athenians did not describe fellow citizens who disclaim an interest in politics as minding their own business. Rather, he said, they had no business at all in Athens.[1] Interest and engagement in the city's public affairs were part of the make-up of Athenian citizenship.

Twenty-five hundred years later, we acknowledge the vast gulf between an ancient city-state and a modern federation occupying half a continent, but we are drawn to an interest common to both: the attachments, rights, and obligations of citizenship. In *Citizenship, Diversity, and Pluralism*[2] the editors and contributors – this writer among them – explored what Alan Cairns described as the vertical and horizontal dimensions of citizenship as a linking mechanism binding citizens to the state and to one another.[3] The volume "assesses the transformation of these two dimensions of citizenship in increasingly diverse and plural modern societies."[4] Nearly two decades later, this process continues and its historical challenges have been joined by new ones, including a decline of trust in institutions and in those who lead them; technological changes that are outpacing our capacity to manage them;[5] emerging issues in migration and immigration; and the rise of populism. The question we encounter is whether the cumulative effects of these and other influences have altered our understanding of citizenship and of our country.

I can recall reminders of my citizenship, some of which would have been shared with other Canadians of my generation. I remember pride, as a child in the 1950s, when my country rolled out a prototype of the most advanced aircraft in the world – the Avro Arrow – and I remember disappointment when its production was cancelled. As an undergraduate student in the 1960s, I was among nascent Canadian nationalists concerned about large numbers of US professors in our universities; we feared that they might substitute American values for Canadian ones. I joined those pondering the great existential question, "What does Quebec want?" and worried about the formation of a political party determined to pursue its sovereignty. I was relieved that my military experience was in the Prince Edward Island Regiment Band and not as a conscript in the Vietnam War. I was impressed that my country was able to implement universal medical care, and I welcomed our evolution as a pluralist state – one less preoccupied by the dichotomous relationship between French and English. I enjoyed hockey, though I lacked the skill to play the game, and I had the typical Canadian consciousness of our vast geography, though it far exceeded personal experience. In summary, reminders of my Canadian-ness, and of the connections and attachments it brings, were common and powerful.

What are the connections and attachments referenced by our Canadian citizenship today? Are its vertical and horizontal dimensions as spoken of by Cairns still in place? Have they been replaced by contemporary equivalents, or supplanted by a more global citizenship? Or have they been attenuated without replacement and with implications for the future that require our attention? These are the questions that provoke this study.

I must acknowledge a burgeoning modern literature on citizenship that attests to changing thought regarding its features and status. In contemplating this book it was not my goal to add to this literature but to follow up on my work with Cairns and colleagues nearly a quarter of a century ago. My concern is not with the concept of citizenship in general; it is with the influences acting upon Canadian citizenship and with its vitality and future. I began the project with the hypothesis that there are growing centrifugal pressures that are changing, perhaps diminishing, our sense of what it means to be Canadian. These pressures may have been ameliorated in the short term by the pandemic but they will return and perhaps intensify when it recedes.

I must acknowledge, too, that I am indebted to several people for their contributions to this project. Michael Atkinson nudged me in the direction of the topic and assisted by responding to ideas and queries along the way. I also received assistance and encouragement from Michael Finley, Richard Florizone, Frank Harvey, Mona Holmlund, Margaret Kierylo, J.R. Miller, Lea Pennock, and David Smith. My staff during my interim presidency at Dalhousie (Erin Stewart-Reid, Chloe Westlake, and Robin Beaton) took an early interest in the project and helped me reconnect to the east coast after nearly fifty years in the west. I was assisted in preparing the manuscript for publication by Gail Brennan, Barbara Langhorst, and the late Susan Bertolo.

Almost a decade ago, University of Toronto president David Naylor introduced me to the University of Toronto Press, in particular to John Yates and Dan Quinlan, and it proved to be one of the most fortuitous introductions in my life. This is the third volume I have published with this excellent organization, and I am grateful for its exemplary standards, professionalism, and support. I was particularly fortunate to work with editor Dan Quinlan on all three books. His comments and advice were invariably wise, and his encouragement helped me in completing this and the previous volumes. It would be my wish for all writers that they have an editor of his calibre by their side.

Leah Connor led the production process for the press; Matthew Kudelka contributed an excellent proofread; Stephanie Mazza and Breanna Muir brought their skills in marketing. The press's anonymous peer reviewers, and the Manuscript Review Committee, provided helpful advice that improved the book. To these individuals and to the entire team at UTP, I offer my thanks.

I received inspiration and assistance from my family. I was lucky to be born in Canada to parents Frank and Daphne MacKinnon, who prized higher education. My wife Janice, sons Alan and William, daughter-in-law Anoma Patirana, and granddaughters

Natalie and Caitlin have been supportive. My extended family –
brothers, sisters, nieces, and nephews – contributed to my lifelong
learning. I am grateful to all.

I wrote this book in 2020 and I am conscious of the risks of writing about contentious, changing issues in a contemporary context.
I understand the risks and I bear sole responsibility for the result.

CANADA IN QUESTION

Exploring Our Citizenship in the Twenty-First Century

Introduction

The celebration of diversity has become an article of faith for many Canadians, particularly for those whose voices are prominent in the public commons. Fuelled anecdotally and in popular conversation by a supposed contrast between an American "melting pot" that is assimilationist in nature and Canadian multiculturalism that exalts racial, cultural, and religious differences, this celebration has reached new heights in recent years.

This contrast between the United States and Canada is incomplete if not inapt. In her seminal volume *The Imperative of Integration*,[1] the University of Michigan's Elizabeth Anderson argues that an outcome of American political movements in the 1960s was "American multiculturalism reflected in today's motley celebrations of diversity, multicultural diversity training, and American history textbooks featuring favourable depictions of the achievements of Americans from different shores."[2] She argues that "in our preoccupation with celebrating our particularistic ethno-racial identities, we have forgotten the value of identification with a larger nationwide community"[3] and urges Americans "to restore integration to a central place on our political agenda"[4].

Anderson's appeal may have resonance in Canada. Ours is a big and "unlikely" country[5] said by Prime Minister Justin Trudeau to be the world's first post-national state, one lacking a "core identity or mainstream."[6] He is not alone in this view.[7] We have been ever conscious of the challenge presented by Quebec to ideas of nationwide community and common citizenship, and other regional differences surface occasionally and sometimes sharply. But there are newer influences – present or imminent – that intensify the challenge: the disrupting impacts of globalization; an unresolved question whether Indigenous peoples are citizens, citizens plus,[8] or fellow travellers on a Two Row Wampum journey; and challenges presented by increasing numbers of special interests more committed to their social and online networks than to a broader conversation with their fellow Canadians.

That is the burden of this proposal: to explore our changing Canadian citizenship and ask whether it is sufficiently robust to withstand today's pressures. It will include comparisons, particularly with the United States because of its proximity and similarities. The objectives are to present a twenty-first-century picture of Canadian citizenship; to assess its future prospects; and to ask whether we need to renew our Canadian citizenship in light of the contemporary pressures to which it is being subjected.

This volume has seven chapters. Chapter 1 revisits the horizontal and vertical dimensions of citizenship explored by Alan Cairns to determine the state of their evolution. Using Linda Bosniak's four spheres for exploring citizenship – legal status, rights, political activity, and collective identity and sentiment – we are able to take a snapshot of the current status of Canadian citizenship. But to develop more than a snapshot, we must consider whether the debate on citizenship is changing, particularly with respect to the impact of identity politics, and whether Canadian institutions can respond constructively to its pressures.

The surge in "us versus them" rhetoric noted in the conclusion of chapter 1 is the focus of chapter 2 on populism and the decline in Enlightenment values. Canada has to date escaped the most negative features of populism in its public life, but they may not be far away, and the decline in Enlightenment values is discernible in Canada as in much of the Western world. What does that mean for our citizenship?

Chapters 3 and 4 are about newcomers. Relative to Indigenous peoples, who have made what is now Canada their home for thousands of years, the rest of us are newcomers – some before others, but all within recent centuries or decades. In chapter 3, the relationship between Indigenous peoples and newcomers is explored along with the prospects for reconciliation, and in chapter 4, future newcomers are anticipated as immigrants, refugees, or migrants. Two issues, in particular, are highlighted – global population growth and climate change – including their possible impacts on international migration, with Canada among the preferred destinations.

In chapter 5, we turn to the relationship between economic opportunity and citizenship. The presence of economic opportunity strengthens the ties of citizenship; their absence diminishes them. The fundamentals of the Canadian economy are not strong, and they will be challenged further by the consequences of the pandemic. We must therefore confront two potentially intractable questions: How will Canadians address Richard Saillant's concern about a demographic imbalance that is pulling Canada apart?[9] And can we pursue internal free trade with the same resolution we have brought to the successful negotiation of international trade agreements?

In chapter 6, we turn to our institutions. The pillars of democratic governance in our vast country are being undermined by weaknesses for which reform has been slow in coming and by a general decline in confidence and trust. Can our institutions better serve their historic responsibilities and address the growing pressures on our federation?

Chapter 7 revisits the six previous chapters in search of answers to the inevitable question: what is to be done?

chapter one

Revisiting Vertical and Horizontal Dimensions of Citizenship

Writing in Canada's centennial year about the country's lack of unity and identity, historian Ramsay Cook observed that while Canadians should try to understand themselves, their frame of reference is wrong: "Perhaps instead of constantly deploring our lack of identity, we should attempt to understand and explain the regional, ethnic and class identities that we do have. It might just be that it is in these limited identities that 'Canadianism' is found, and that except for our over-heated nationalist intellectuals, Canadians find this situation quite satisfactory."[1]

More than fifty years later we must question Cook's observation. "Canada does not have a national identity," writes Donald Savoie in 2018, "rather we have a series of provincial identities."[2] We have explored them and other sub-national attachments since Cook's centenary observation though not with results that illuminate what it means to be Canadian. We have endured two Quebec independence referendums the second of which brought the country to the edge of break-up, and there are intermittent and sometimes smouldering resentments elsewhere – particularly in the west – that find expression in secessionist sentiment. Current voices on race and gender have been less dramatic and more focused on their particulars than on citizenship. Discussions of class find contemporary expression in the polarizing language of populism.

Cook's view that a national identity may be discerned through sub-national ones contrasts with Alan Cairn's invitation to explore dimensions of citizenship that bind citizens to the state and to one another, and American scholar Linda Bosniak identifies four distinct spheres in which we might do so: legal status, rights, political activity, and collective identity and sentiment.[3] Each has a history that is distinct to particular societies; the interest here is in their contemporary status in Canada.

We begin with the law. Historically, citizenship has been seen as the business of individual states – "the last bastion of sovereign discretion"[4] – and Canada's Citizenship Act[5] tells us who are citizens, who must be granted citizenship, and how it may be renounced, revoked, or resumed. We also have rights that are core dimensions of our citizenship. The rights to enter and to be in the country are the most basic; we also share the rights enshrined in the Charter of Rights and Freedoms. In what was the most notable modern achievement of our country, the federal and nine provincial governments[6] agreed in 1982 to be bound by a new and comprehensive statement of our rights and freedoms, a sufficient endorsement for it to apply from coast to coast. In brief, the Charter sets out declarations of fundamental freedoms together with democratic, mobility, legal, and equality rights and acknowledges official bilingualism, Aboriginal rights, and Canada's multicultural heritage.

There are limits. Section 1 of the Charter guarantees the enumerated rights and freedoms "subject only to such reasonable limits prescribed by law as can be demonstrably justified in a free and democratic society." The jurisprudence on this section tells us that the bar is high for those seeking to limit our rights and freedoms. Theirs is the burden of making the case, and they must show that a proposed limitation addresses "concerns that are pressing in a free and democratic society" and that it does so proportionately or in measured fashion.

Canadians appreciate the Charter. It has been acclaimed as a centrepiece of our constitution and as a primary reason why the country remains united.[7] In 2014, former minister of justice and attorney general of Canada Irwin Cotler lauded it as "a great addition to Canada's constitution" and one "worth celebrating given its transformative impact not only on our laws, but on our lives."[8] The Charter we share as Canadians is a vital feature of our citizenship.

Bosniak's third sphere of citizenship – political activity – reminds us of the words of Pericles that opened this volume. Engagement in a country's public life has been associated with citizenship over time, and "[the] idea that civic participation in the political community constitutes the core of what we mean by 'citizenship' remains popular."[9] This core idea, this expectation of participation in our public life, is both a vertical and a horizontal dimension of citizenship. It binds citizens to their state and, through the mutuality of this obligation, to one another.

It is an enduring concept though one not often invoked today.[10] Leaders rarely mention common citizenship in the name of national interests. Our decentralized federation elevates local allegiances over national ones. Single-issue proponents are focused on their single issues and not on a broader public discourse. Local or regional claims of social licence are employed in attempts to sidetrack the constitutional rules by which the country is supposed to be governed.[11] One third or more of eligible Canadian voters steer clear of the ballot box when our national governments are chosen.

Canadians may be so preoccupied with their private lives that they pay scant attention to citizenship. They look to personal, social, and community allegiances to express their public impulses and wishes, or they may feel they don't count. Some may not care. Political parties reflect this decline or indifference. Fault lines in the 2019 federal election emphasized predicable labels and differences on issues; the only party that invoked citizenship was the Bloc Québécois, which has no interest in Canadian citizenship, only a Quebec one. The result is a divided country: the Liberal government lacks House of Commons representation between Winnipeg and Vancouver and faces a resurgent, unambiguously separatist Bloc. Our common citizenship is once again in question.

Bosniak's fourth sphere is collective identity and sentiment, "affective ties of identification and solidarity."[12] What does Canadian citizenship mean to Canadians? The question can be answered in an empirical manner and answers will be as varied as those who offer them. While our collective experiences point to sentiments that are shared, each of us has had other experiences that are unique to our time, place, and circumstances in the

world – our "positionality," in social science parlance. Yet sentiment can be measured, and it is instructive to turn to opinion polls
on the subject.

The country fared well in a 2017 Ipsos poll commissioned
by Global News.[13] High percentages of Canadians were well-
disposed to our social services, particularly Medicare. Four-fifths
of our number attributed importance to our tolerance and multicultural diversity. Progress was cited in gender equality, overall quality of life, and the country's pathway to becoming a great
place to live. A 2016 study led by Quebec pollster Jean-Marc Léger
found high overlap in the attitudes of English Canadians and
French Quebecers,[14] and there is little indication that newer Canadians feel differently about the country than those who have been
here for a long time.

Canada fares well, too, when compared with other countries. In
2018, the *Globe and Mail*'s John Ibbitson summarized our relative
well-being:

> Canada is the most inclusive and tolerant country in the world (Ipsos),
> the second best place in the world to live, after Switzerland (*U.S. News
> and World Report*). Canadians are among the happiest people on Earth
> (ranked seventh according to a United Nations report), in part because
> we live in one of the safest places on Earth (ranked sixth according to
> the Global Peace Index) and our cities enjoy the highest quality of life in
> the Western hemisphere (Mercer Quality of Living Survey).[15]

Important measures are missing from the comparison (competitiveness, productivity, and business investment) that raise questions about the sustainability of these favourable rankings; even
so, our good fortune remains comparatively high.

Patriotism is an expression of sentiment, and while Canadians
may not be exuberant in their patriotism – except when their sports
teams participate in international competition – their pride in
country is robust.[16] At one time sung in tepid, self-conscious fashion, the National Anthem is now performed in several languages
with the sensitivity the music deserves. And in the years since 1965
when the Maple Leaf replaced the Red Ensign as the national flag,

it has become a widely recognized, indeed ubiquitous symbol of Canada, appearing on clothes, backpacks, pandemic face masks, and other articles or places to which it can be affixed. Gone are the days recounted by Margaret Atwood when the country's "central symbol" was survival.[17] It is now the Maple Leaf.

The political class fares less well in our surveys. In the 2017 Ipsos poll, more than one third of Canadians indicated that the country's form of government was the worst thing about the country. Similar numbers felt that our political leaders were worse or much worse than they were twenty-five years ago. Canada is not alone in this respect. In a 2016 survey, a majority of people in twenty-five countries surveyed – including Canada – thought their country to be on the wrong track.[18] In the wake of a 2019 election campaign that one expert described as among the "more vituperative" in recent history,[19] it is unlikely that the numbers have improved since these polls were taken.

The Crown, the House of Commons, and the Senate comprise Canada's parliament. The Crown is a public institution of constitutional stature as well as ceremonial importance. But there is declining attachment to the monarchy. In a recent Angus Reid poll, two thirds of the respondents said the British Crown "is losing or has lost relevance in their lives,"[20] and nearly half said "Canada should not continue as a constitutional monarchy for generations and generations to come."[21] Affection and admiration for Elizabeth II endure, though less so for her successors and other members of the Royal Family.

If we were sceptical about Ramsay Cook's suggestions about Canadian identity, we may also have reservations about Donald Savoie's view that we have only provincial ones. Our citizenship has legal substance, and Canadians enjoy a high level of rights protection. Engagement in the country's public life may be wanting, and we might hope for higher levels of respect for governance and leadership, but Canadians in general are conscious of their advantages and positively disposed toward their country.

Though Linda Bosniak helps us frame a snapshot of our citizenship, her four spheres do not capture the moving picture. For that we must return to the evolution of the horizontal and vertical dimensions of citizenship. Alan Cairns reminds us that the "contemporary question is ... whether the practice of citizenship still has the ability to link members of a society in a relation of rights and obligations to the state"[22] and that the contemporary challenge is "finding a basis for cohesion without smothering difference."[23] To respond to his question and to address his challenge we must turn to the subject of identity politics.

American literature on this subject is of interest. Harvard University's Steven Pinker tells us that identity politics "is the syndrome in which people's beliefs and interests are assumed to be determined by their membership in groups, particularly their sex, race, sexual orientation and disability status."[24] Its roots lie in the combating of discrimination and disadvantage, but "when it spreads beyond [these targets] it is an enemy of reason and Enlightenment values."[25] Columbia University's Mark Lilla would say that battle has been joined.[26] With American liberalism in his sights, he argues that in recent decades, liberals have thrown themselves "into the movement politics of identity, losing a sense of what we share as citizens and what binds us as a nation."[27] Ironically, this development has reinforced the individualism that is at the core of Republicans' thinking. Originally concerned with the rights of women and African-Americans, left-wing identity politics had by the 1980s "given way to a pseudo-politics of self-regard and increasingly narrow and exclusionary self-definition that is now cultivated in our colleges and universities":[28] "The main result has been to turn young people back onto themselves, rather than turning them outward to the wider world. It has left them unprepared to think about the common good and what must be done practically to secure it – especially the hard and unglamorous task of persuading people very different from themselves to join a common effort."[29]

This process may have been accelerated by social media. Queen's University professor William Cannon worries that Facebook and other social media platforms "have conditioned our students to expect solutions to complex problems to be deliverable in 15-second sound bites; dissuaded students from reading more than 140 characters at a time ... and truly robbed many students of the capacity to think through problems ... on their own"[30] rather than through search engines or crowdsourcing.[31] *New York Times* columnist Roger Cohen shares these concerns about social media and points to its capacity for distortion: "Facebook reaches about one-third of humanity. It is more powerful than any political party – and it's full of untruths, bigotry and nonsense."[32]

Stanford University's Francis Fukuyama advanced the debate in his 2018 volume *Identity: The Demand for Dignity and the Politics of Resentment*.[33] He sees American national identity as under attack from both the right and the left – from newly emergent white nationalist voices on the right and identity politics on the left[34] – and he worries that "state breakdown and failure" could eventually result.[35] He joins Cannon and Cohen in identifying the role that social media plays in this attack: it "has succeeded in accelerating the fragmentation of liberal societies by playing into the hands of identity groups. It connected like-minded people with one another, freed from the tyranny of geography. It permitted them to communicate, and to wall themselves off from people and views that they didn't like."[36]

New York University's Kwame Anthony Appiah suggests that we can break down these walls through a deeper and more nuanced understanding of identity.[37] Our identities can be "forms of confinement,"[38] but they can also "expand our horizons to communities larger than ones we personally inhabit."[39] He aspires to see our common humanity rise above all.[40]

The Canadian experience has not been so pointedly stated, but the issues are familiar. Multiculturalism has long been official Canadian policy, and has enjoyed powerful intellectual support,[41] but some have worried that it could evolve toward multinationalism. In 2005 a published anthology celebrating the work of Alan Cairns addressed the evolution of identity politics and set the context for what has followed.[42] Cairns's wariness of identity politics is illustrated by his comparison of moderate and strong versions of the concept.[43] Common to both is the concern – well-grounded in historical experience – that "when policy is discussed and decisions are taken that affect the life chances of citizens, the identities that are not represented will be overlooked, misunderstood, or shabbily treated."[44] The moderate version of identity politics "sensitizes society to expressions of difference that historically were suppressed, concealed or unvoiced"[45] and requires accommodation of them in exploring the whole of our citizenship.

The strong version of identity politics is what troubled Cairns, for it challenges representation and representative democracy: A cannot represent B because of their differences. "You have to be one to understand one or to represent one":[46] "The strong version encourages charges of 'voice appropriation' when 'outsiders' express opinions about experiences they have not had or identities they lack ... The resultant constraints on discussion inhibit the growth of the mutual understanding that contributes to social cohesion and supports a unifying citizenship."[47]

Cairns's overarching concern was Canada's evolution toward a multinational (as distinct from a multicultural) society, one that lacked an "institutional framework for its expression."[48] Such a framework might not be possible within a united country. "Can the centre hold?," he asked, and he feared the answer might be no.

The rebuttal comes in part from Peter Russell, who acknowledges that Canada is a multinational democracy and offers a contrasting view of its citizenship: "The bond that ties the citizens of [a multinational democracy] together is not a common sense of civic identity but participation in a common political space in which, through democratic discussion and debate ... they negotiate the terms on which they are willing to share citizenship."[49] The Charter recognizes multinational citizenship for Indigenous nations and, arguably, for the Québécois as well and is potentially "an instrument of citizenization for all of Canada's peoples."[50]

A more trenchant critique comes from Alexandra Dobrowolsky and Richard Devlin,[51] who write that the limitations of Cairns's work arise from "the call to reason rather than passion; the need for stability, predictability and coherence rather than precariousness, provisionality, and experimentation; the privileging of the institutional over the non-institutional; and finally, the preference for sameness over difference."[52] They contemplate a sidetracking of our institutions that would have been anathema to Cairns: "the choice is not necessarily between the stability of conventional political structures and political chaos but between the hegemony of our traditional, fossilized, and exclusionary political structures and the emancipatory potential of ... political forums that facilitate change."[53] It is *non*-institutional politics that point to future change, and because Cairns does not recognize the legitimacy of identity politics,[54] he "ultimately prioritizes sameness over difference in his call for a common citizenship."[55]

The institutional framework that so concerned Alan Cairns is that of a modern democratic state within which reason, stability, and coherence should be compelling attributes and values. Avigail Eisenberg and Will Kymlicka turned their attention to this framework in *Identity Politics in the Public Realm: Bringing Institutions Back In:*[56]

> Although identity politics is not new, it is surely true that the past three decades have witnessed an intensification and multiplication of such struggles. Long-standing identity groups have become repoliticized ... to contest the terms of citizenship ... These older cleavages have been joined by a raft of new identity movements – such as those defined by sexual orientation or disability – many of which have formed organized political movements and have made visible political claims to recognition and accommodation for the first time.[57]

Like Appiah, Eisenberg and Kymlicka see a creative potential in identity politics, so the question for them "is not whether identity politics is to be avoided but rather how public institutions respond to this form of politics and what role they play in either exacerbating or mitigating the risks associated with it."[58] Their interest is in "a progressive politics of identity"[59] and in how to promote such politics while reducing or containing its negative impacts. They identify some themes that emerged from the international discussion they led: one is that history matters, albeit for both good and ill. The good relates to the historical foundation for organizing and engaging with identity groups; the negative, to a risk of rigidity in identity group definition and leadership. Another theme – the most striking, in their view – is the democratic framework. "The capacity of minority groups to influence state policies and to challenge state assumptions about the nature of their identities and interests depends on whether the governance of identity is democratized."[60] When it is, "groups have been able to negotiate claims democratically in a peaceful manner that exhibits a willingness to compromise rather than simply engage in inflated identity rhetoric and non-negotiable posturing."[61]

Still another theme is what Eisenberg and Kymlicka refer to as institutional reflexivity[62] or awareness. Identity claims are nothing new to legislatures and courts, and they can be addressed well or poorly depending on the motivations of their actors:

> Where identity politics are interpreted with emancipatory aims in mind, such as responding to discrimination or historical disadvantage, the risks and challenges of identity politics are easier to meet. Where institutions are instead motivated by their own strategic concerns – such as protecting the colonial privilege of one group, enjoying favourable status with particular allies, or bending to the demands of particular interest groups – identity politics become distorted and confining.[63]

For Kymlicka and Kathryn Walker, Canada is a test case for what they (and Appiah before them) view as rooted cosmopolitanism,[64] a concept that links the local attachments of national citizenship to the imperative of conforming our behaviours to a "normative conception of global community, responsibility and governance."[65] The two are consistent, and indeed, national citizenship can *advance* cosmopolitanism – "an exciting idea, not least for Canadians, given the deep diversity and plurality of our cultures and communities."[66] Whether the idea is viable is another matter. Robert Paehlke uses Canada's failure to live up to its commitment to addressing climate change to illustrate that "the problem is not that Canadians' expressed cosmopolitan values are illusory, but rather that they have been undermined by a range of political and institutional factors, such as federalism."[67] While Paehlke reminds us of "the vast gulf that can separate expressed cosmopolitan values and effective political action,"[68] his criticism of federalism is inapt. Our federal state has adapted to emergencies or other extraordinary circumstances before climate change,[69] and while identifying the correct combination of emission reductions, green technologies, and adaptations necessary to address it may be the greatest challenge of all, it is not one solely for the national government. It requires cooperative federalism as well as rooted cosmopolitanism that engages all levels of government.[70]

Conclusion

In a mature democracy such as Canada, institutions matter. They provide the constitutional framework for our federation, and they are the only legitimate arbiters of our political differences, including those related to identity. Our citizenship matters because it informs expectations of ourselves, other Canadians, and our country and its place in the world. Its modern evolution clarifies the questions now before us. What is the present state of our citizenship? Do we approach the question in Cairns's terms, or has the debate shifted onto new ground of multinationalism and identity? Do the institutions of our parliamentary democracy accommodate the shifting ground of the debate, or are they "fossilized, exclusionary,"[71] and sidetracked by it? If they are, can they be "brought back in"?[72] Is rooted cosmopolitanism a viable political project?

The wider context for our discussion may influence its direction. In recent years Amnesty International has pointed to a surge of "us versus them" rhetoric around the world.[73] Margaret MacMillan draws upon contemporary as well as earlier examples to remind us that history "can be dangerous when it is used to set peoples against each other."[74] Canada has its share of "us versus them" rhetoric and advocacy, and this makes a search for dimensions of citizenship that emphasize social cohesion and civic identity all the more compelling. Whether such a search can succeed in the Canada of 2020 and beyond is a question that will remain with us in the chapters that follow.

chapter two

Populism, Enlightenment Values, and Citizenship

Warnings from Amnesty International, Margaret MacMillan, and other serious voices that "us versus them" politics have not reached their present level of intensity since the 1930s should not be lightly dismissed.[1] That decade ended in world war, and while a third global war is unlikely, economic and social malaise is less remote. The capacity to avert them depends on robust democracy, mature institutions, leadership capable of generating common will, and populations amenable to joining in common cause. Populism raises questions about whether this capacity exists and is sustainable.

It is understatement to say that the word is not used with precision. According to *New York Times* columnist Roger Cohen,

> populists may be authoritarians, ethnonationalists, nativists, leftists, rightists, xenophobes, proto-fascists, fascists, autocrats, losers from globalization, moneyed provocateurs, conservatives, socialists, and just plain and unhappy or frustrated or bored people – anyone, from the crazed to the rational, from the racist to the tolerant, energized by social media to declare the liberal democratic rules-based consensus that has broadly prevailed since the end of the Cold War is not for them.[2]

This wide eligibility for the label is explained by Cas Mudde and Cristobal Rovira Kaltwasser in their description of populism as "a thin-centred ideology":[3] "expressions of populism are almost always combined with very different (thin and full) ideologies such as conservatism, liberalism, nativism or 'Americanismo.'

This implies that in the real world there are few, if any, pure forms of populism (in isolation) but, rather, subtypes of it, which show a specific articulation of certain ideological features."[4]

There is agreement, however, that populism "is predicated upon the positing of an antagonistic relationship between two collective identities: 'the people' and 'the elites.'"[5] Harvard University's Norm Gidron and Bart Bonikowski "focus on three main conceptual approaches that emerge out of the political science and sociology literature on the topic"; they define populism, respectively, as "an ideology, a discursive style, and a form of political mobilization."[6] With respect to the first, populism "is first and foremost a set of ideas caused by an antagonism between the people and the elite, as well as the primacy of popular sovereignty, whereby the virtuous general will is placed in opposition to the moral corruption of elite actors."[7] With the second, populism as discursive style, we hear the rhetoric of "us versus them" from left, right, or in between, depending on context. The third, populism as political strategy, "comprises three variants that focus on different aspects of the subject: policy choices, political organization, and forms of mobilization."[8]

It is clear that the three conceptual approaches are not mutually exclusive, that they "have their differences, but also points of connection and overlap."[9] In addition to providing a framework for populism, Gidron and Bonikowski caution researchers – and, we might add, everyone – to be "as explicit and precise as possible in their definition of populism."[10]

We should note as one of its important features that populism "is typically critical of representation and anything that mediates the relation between the people and their leader or government."[11] In a contest between the people and elites, the people will count representatives, officials, and bureaucrats among the elites and therefore among their political foes. This has two consequences: first, it tends to sideline the institutions of governance in which representatives, officials, and bureaucrats are engaged; and second, it attributes an elevated status to the leader, who pays scant attention to legal, constitutional, or administrative constraints on his power. Implementing populist will is what matters, not adhering to the protocols of democracy.

Gidron and Bonikowski's second conceptual approach – populism as discursive style – is developed by Elena Block and Ralph Negrine, who offer "a critical framework that integrates three key categories to identify and analyze the most relevant features of the populist communication style: identity, rhetoric and use of the media."[12] Identity is key to the role played by populist leaders in the construction of "the people," a notion that loosely brings together all those with "unfulfilled demands, a group destined to break the status quo, take power from the ruling elite (the Other) and build a new ... populist order."[13] Their rhetoric "involves adversarial, emotional, patriotic and abrasive speech through which they connect with the discontented."[14] "They use multiple channels of political communication to transmit their messages and connect with their publics."[15]

The third conceptual approach outlined by Gidron and Bonikowski – political strategy – is the operational one, and here we note the argument of Michael Hatherall that when populists acquire executive power, "they will be driven to align their strategic choices to their populist narrative":[16]

> It is no surprise ... that President Trump's most important foreign policy decisions and statements have directly aligned with his campaign narrative of U.S. leaders making bad deals with foreign countries. The decision to pull out of multilateral agreements such as the Trans-Pacific Partnership and the Paris Agreement, the imposition of trade tariffs and efforts to unsettle the existing trade relationship with China, belligerent language towards traditional allies and constant criticism of domestic elites who allowed supposed bad deals to occur, all represent an alignment of a populist narrative with grand strategy.[17]

The mobilization of populist supporters has led the University of Zurich's Simon Bornschier to ask two questions of interest here: What leads voters to support populism? And who are the populist voters?[18] In answer to the first question, we are informed that populist voters "seem to have a troubled relationship not only with the political system, but also with their subjective social status."[19] Studies show "that populist attitudes are embedded in deep feelings of discontent."[20] In answering the second question, we learn that "it is not the worst off that develop populist attitudes."[21] Populism emerges from those of varying resources "who angrily demand their share from an elite that is seen as self-serving and unresponsive."[22]

Bornschier's questions point to the debate about the potentially positive and negative outcomes of populism:

> Populism might increase representation and give a voice to groups of citizens that do not feel heard by the current political elite. Populism might broaden the attention for issues that are not in the mainstream news. Populism might mobilize groups of people that have felt on the fringe of the political system. Populism might improve the responsiveness of the political system by making actors and parties align their policies more with the "wishes of the people." Populism might be a refreshing wakeup call to power holders, prompting periodic reflections on their conduct and elitism.[23]

But populism also "constitutes a fundamental challenge to the institutions and values of liberal democracy."[24] It may "curb minority rights" or "use the electoral mandate to erode independent institutions that are considered cornerstones of existing democracies, like the courts or the free media."[25] It may "lead to political tribalism, which impedes civil discourse and discourages political compromise."[26] Populism rejects pluralism – an understanding "that values are often in conflict" and that "demands of justice, fairness, freedom and equality ... often point in different directions. There's no universally accepted ordering of such values so good people will disagree on what's right. The purpose of liberal democracy is to accommodate these disagreements and let people live together peaceably despite them."[27]

The practice of populism further undermines liberal democracy. Moises Naim observes that "despite differences in culture, history, political systems, or the economic circumstances of the countries where populism is now being deployed, populist leaders resort to the same tactics"[28]: they practise divide and conquer; they magnify their country's problems and criminalize the opposition; they play up external threats while claiming that foreign enemies are in the midst of those at home; they glorify the military, discredit experts, and attack the media.

Populist leadership has been identified in several countries. According to one report,[29] there have been forty-six populist leaders or political parties that have led thirty-three countries between 1990 and 2018 – a fivefold increase in numbers over those same years. Originally most prevalent in Latin America and in Eastern and Central Europe, it is now also found in Asia and Western Europe. "Watershed political events in recent years – the election of President Donald Trump ... the Brexit vote, the electoral success of Italy's Five Star Movement, Brazil's sudden lurch to the right with the election of President Jair Bolsonaro, the doubling of support for populist parties across Europe – have brought the word 'populism' out of the annals of academic journals and into the headlines."[30]

Those headlines became more disturbing in the final weeks of the Trump administration, when thousands of his followers gathered in Washington as Congress prepared to confirm Biden's election win. Incited by the outgoing president, the gathering turned into a mob bent on infiltrating, mocking, and disrupting the institutions and processes of American democracy. This was populism run amok, inspired by the nation's populist-in-chief, and its consequences were serious: casualties among the mob and those deployed to resist it, as well as appeals for Trump's ouster two weeks before the inauguration of his successor. As of this writing, the extent and duration of the damage is not fully known, but the episode is a striking demonstration of the dangers of the us-versus-them thinking that is so common today.

Canadians have no reason to be complacent about populism. Our decentralized federation, the absence of anti-state public sentiment, and our relatively successful emergence from the 2007–8 recession[31] may explain why it has not gained the traction in Canada that we have seen elsewhere. But there have been populist influences in our history,[32] and some have anticipated the emergence of its more severe modern variant.[33] Though its expression to date has been subtle, the "thin-centred ideology" may yet surface in the mainstream, particularly in concert with a decline in Enlightenment values.

The legacy of the Enlightenment that dominated European ideas from the 1700s to the late 1900s was "a cornucopia of ideas, some of them contradictory, but four themes tie them together: reason, science, humanism and progress."[34] Reason takes the lead here and is the enabler of the others:

> If there's anything the Enlightenment thinkers had in common, it was an insistence that we energetically apply the standard of reason to understanding our world, and not fall back on generators of delusion like faith, dogma, revelation, authority, charisma, mysticism, divination, visions, gut feelings, or the hermeneutic[s] parsing of sacred texts ... The deliberate application of reason was necessary precisely because our common habits of thought are not particularly reasonable.[35]

Steven Pinker believes that Enlightenment themes – and values – continue to be confronted by human inclinations for "loyalty to tribe, deference to authority, magical thinking, the blaming of misfortune on evildoers"[36] and that they "are treated by today's intellectuals with indifference, skepticism and sometimes contempt."[37] Underlying this observation is Pinker's rejection of a right wing–left wing dichotomy and the ideologies along the spectrum. "A more rational approach to politics is to treat societies as ongoing experiments and open-mindedly learn the best practices, whichever part of the spectrum they come from. The empirical picture at present suggests that people flourish most in liberal democracies with a mixture of civic norms, guaranteed rights, market freedom, social spending, and judicious regulation."[38] But this picture is at odds with ideologues and with "religious, political and cultural pessimists who insist that Western civilization is in terminal decline."[39] Pinker argues that the evidence supports the opposite conclusion. "The Enlightenment has worked – perhaps the greatest story seldom told."[40] And because its achievements are often denied or taken for granted, its ideals need renewed defence for the twenty-first century.

Pinker is the latest celebrant of the Enlightenment. Earlier ones included Albert Saloman, who wrote of "the orthodoxies, fanaticisms and prejudices ... which need enlightened reexamination" and argued that the "desire for enlightened vigilance and praise of the Enlightenment are appropriate in the contemporary age of irrational modes of thinking and acting."[41] More recently, Anthony Pagden has shown "how Enlightenment concepts directly influenced modern culture, making possible a secular, tolerant, and above all, cosmopolitan world,"[42] and Tzvetan Todorov has praised the Enlightenment's "celebration of plurality, of difference, of the idea that debate is healthy and productive."[43]

The counter-arguments begin with the claim that Enlightenment thinking is monolithic on the subject of religion. Emory University's Dominic Erdozain writes that "Christians are taught to despise the Enlightenment. It is hard to find a theologian with a good word for this era of rational presumption ... The Enlightenment is the sin of the modern; the chimera of crass autonomy ... The picture is sharpened by a secular literature that celebrates the Enlightenment as a brave emancipation from theological tutelage: a defiant obituary for an expired God."[44]

Erdozain argues that in fact, the Enlightenment "was as religious as anything that came before it – a time of spiritual awakening as well as criticism and doubt."[45] While secularism is among its credos, we learn from Charles Taylor that this does not mean the disappearance of religion; once freed from the strictures of fundamentalism, secularism can be accompanied by robust spiritual pluralism.[46]

The counter-argument is not limited to religion, and debate on the legacy of the Enlightenment "and its ideological child, liberalism"[47] will continue. The interest here is in the impact of non-liberal critics of the Enlightenment (from the left and the right) on the future of liberal thought and its political expression, liberal democracy. From the left, according to Stephen Bonner, Enlightenment values have "come under assault" from "anarchists, communitarians, post-modernists, half-hearted liberals and authoritarian socialists":[48] "Ideals long associated with reactionary movements – the privileging of experience over reasoning, national or ethnic identity over internationalism and cosmopolitanism, the community over the individual, custom over innovation, myth over science – have entered the thinking of the American left ... The collapse of intellectual coherence on the left reflects the collapse of a purposeful politics from the left."[49]

From the right, again according to Bonner, "anti-Enlightenment and anti-modern prejudices" persist as conservative thinkers "obsess about sexual licence and the decline of family values, cultural 'nihilism' and the loss of tradition, tolerance for divergent life-styles and the erosion of national identity."[50]

If this case for the rise of populism and the fall of Enlightenment values is sound, then we must consider its implications for Canada and for our citizenship. We note again that populism has not gained the traction in this country that it has in some other Western nations. However, its sentiments are sometimes heard, and may grow, and so our interest in the subject is not misplaced.

What do populism and weakened Enlightenment values mean for pluralism, solidarity, and public discourse? The two in combination are what first catch our attention. Either – by itself – may undermine liberal democracy, but in tandem the threat is increased because each magnifies the other: populism accelerates a decline in Enlightenment values and is in turn strengthened by a flight from reason, science, and humanism.

Pluralism is essential to democratic governance of a large federation with a number of provinces and regions, and a multicultural population, but differences can be submerged within "the people" in the populist contest between them and elites. A growth in populism makes complex societies more susceptible to factions arrayed against one another and rulers they perceive as controlling their lives. Fragmentation into groups of like-minded individuals, strategizing with one another on social media, and turning away from those with whom they disagree, diminishes the wide, continuing, and often difficult conversations necessary for democratic life.

To the extent that populism, properly understood, has been contained in Canada, it is not posing a threat to our liberal democracy and the pluralism on which it rests. Multiculturalism has been a

Canadian reality for decades, and its pluralist foundation is understood and generally accepted. We cannot be as sanguine about a decline in Enlightenment values. The threats to them are as discernible in Canada as they are elsewhere. Especially troubling is the threat to Enlightenment values in our universities, where some students and faculty treat those who disagree with them as not simply in error but in sin: "I am right, you are wrong and therefore a wrongdoer." They are not above threats, nor are they above shouting down those with whom they disagree in efforts to silence them and to embed their own views on social justice in university policy. If Enlightenment values are not as protected as they should be in our universities, we cannot expect them to flourish more widely.

Solidarity and public discourse suffer as well. We should be cautious in our use of the word solidarity, for its meaning depends on speaker and context. Here we are interested in what it means for us to say "We, as Canadians." For some, it may mean nothing: they see the country in terms that leave them unattached to it except for the convenience of holding its passport and whatever of its benefits may fall their way. Some may embrace the cancel culture that sees our history in terms of the villainies they attribute to its principal actors and even to fellow citizens, overlooking their more complicated lives and legacies. For Canadian citizenship to endure, however, most of us must have a positive attachment to the country. Attachments will differ in kind and intensity but they have to be present. We asked an important question in chapter 1: what does Canadian citizenship mean to Canadians? And there is evidence that most Canadians have positive views of the country and take pride in their citizenship. That is solidarity enough, but it must be sustained and encouraged to withstand the decline in Enlightenment values.

Populism and declining Enlightenment values undermine public discourse too. We know that "the communicative tools for spreading populist ideas are just as central as the populist ideas themselves."[51] As previously noted, populist rhetoric features "adversarial, emotional, patriotic and abrasive speech"[52] that inspires or moves the converted but is obnoxious and often crude to others. In a context of weakening Enlightenment values, its simplified and exaggerated messaging divides listeners instead of bringing them together.

Conclusion

We must contemplate the consequences of an end to a liberal democratic rules-based social order. What would take its place? We don't know, of course, but we can foresee a more authoritarian successor rooted in the ideology of left or right. This is the place to which populists and deniers of Enlightenment values would take us, and both the journey and the destination must be resisted.

The first step in resisting them is to understand their origins. Why do supporters of populism believe themselves to be sidelined and ignored? Why do many people turn away from reason when it has been the foundation of modernity? Why (as Pinker asks) do some in our universities – supposedly citadels of reason – treat Enlightenment values with disdain? Where have our democratic institutions fallen short in their representative and delibera-tive responsibilities? We need serious, open, and evidence-based debate on these questions even though the questions themselves point to conditions that make that debate less likely to occur.

We have seen that populism is less demonstrable in Canada than in many other countries. However, it may yet gain more vis-ible traction here and threaten pluralism, solidarity, and public discourse. Combined with a decline in Enlightenment values it threatens our democracy. Unless that threat is averted our citizen-ship too will be undermined.

chapter three

Indigenous Peoples and Citizenship

It is not possible to undertake a broad inquiry of Canadian citizenship without considering Indigenous peoples in a contemporary context. That task requires sensitivity to what social scientists call "positionality" – a term that reminds us of a dictum attributed to Nelson Mandela that where you stand depends on where you sit. Acknowledging that the sensitivity of the issues discussed in this chapter may lead readers to inquire about my positionality, I outline it here. I am a seventy-three-year-old non-Indigenous male, a lawyer and former law professor whose first academic appointment was as a lecturer in the inaugural Program of Legal Studies for Native People launched at the University of Saskatchewan in 1973. That experience led to my determination – later as a law professor and dean – to attract Indigenous students to the study of law and to put in place supports to better ensure their success. When I was a university president, attracting and supporting Indigenous students was among my highest priorities – the great social imperative of the twenty-first century, as I described it in countless speeches. The number of Indigenous students at the University of Saskatchewan has risen from a few hundred to more than three thousand today. I do not claim credit for this, but I was among those who contributed.

At many of the Indigenous ceremonies I attended, I was proud to wear the eagle-feather headdress presented to me by Indigenous leaders in Saskatchewan to recognize the university's commitment and progress in this area. Upon my retirement, I was gratified to see the Gordon Oakes Red Bear Student Centre – designed by the great Indigenous architect Douglas Cardinal – under construction at a prominent site on the university campus.

This chapter constitutes my attempt to understand the relationship between Indigenous peoples and Canadian citizenship for myself and, by extension, for my readers. I have learned from the insights of Indigenous scholars – Gordon Christie, John Borrows, Glen Coulthard, Aaron Mills, Joshua Ben David Nichols, Leanne Betasamosake Simpson, and Heidi Kiiwetinepinesiik Stark – as well as many non-Indigenous ones. This chapter, I hope, will be counted as a contribution to an important debate about our citizenship.

In Ottawa's Confederation Park, the National Aboriginal Veterans Monument commemorates the service of thousands of Indigenous men and women who were members of Canada's armed forces during two world wars and one in Korea. Since then, many Indigenous ceremonies have devoted pride of place to veterans in attendance, who are distinguishable by their berets with regimental insignia attached. There are fewer of them now, and in time all will have passed into history, but in wartime their numbers – said to have been about 12,000 – were impressive, particularly so given that they were drawn from a small percentage of the country's population.[1] The numbers were impressive, too, because of the Canada from which they came and to which the survivors returned. The country's treatment of Indigenous peoples has been the greatest blight on its history, and it would not have been surprising if more of them had turned away from wartime service.

The relationship did not begin this way. Historian J.R. Miller analyses its initial and subsequent phases in *Skyscrapers Hide the Heavens: A History of Native–Newcomer Relations in Canada*.[2] In the first phase, "Europeans came to North America in pursuit of goals that could not be reached without First Nations cooperation,"[3] and in the early period after first contact the relationship "was one of mutual benefit."[4] Theirs was a commercial liaison centred on trade – mainly an exchange of iron to be used in weapons and utensils for beaver furs to be used in European clothing. It worked for both, so their relations "were not only mutually beneficial but

also harmonious."[5] The First Nations were the "dominant partner,"[6] and their involvement was seen "as a means rather than an
impediment to the realization of European objectives."[7] However,
destructive impacts would follow:

> Undoubtedly the new technology based on iron greatly improved
> everyday life and hunting, but it also made warfare more destructive.
> French brandy also was a popular means of recreation, but it wreaked
> a fearful havoc at times. More serious still were the scourges of disease
> and religion. One killed the bodies of thousands of Indigenous peoples;
> the other eroded the belief systems that were both a reflection and a
> support of their relationship with the cosmos and each other.[8]

In addition to commercial competition in the fur trade from
which Indigenous peoples continued to benefit, the eighteenth
century brought a struggle between Britain and France for control of North America in which First Nations fought on both sides.
"This second phase of Native–European relations, the era of alli-
ance, produced important developments of great relevance for
both First Nations and Euro-Canadians in later ages."[9] First among
these was the Royal Proclamation of 1763, which "in the short term
meant maintaining Indigenous support for Britain by not threatening their lands, and in the longer term formed part of the foundation of claims for land and self-government."[10]

The nineteenth century brought the third phase of the relationship, one that saw an end to mutuality as new Canadians, who
now outnumbered Indigenous peoples, increasingly saw them as
a problem, "an impediment that had to be cleared away"[11] to make
room for settlers and their settlements. Ominously, new Canadians came to see Native Americans "not as culturally different but
as racially distinct or 'other.'" The change was important: "seeing
Indigenous people as racially separate and alien would underlie
much mistreatment of the Native Americans by the state in the
nineteenth century"[12] – and, we might add, in the twentieth century as well.

The fourth phase of the relationship continues to the present day and is incomplete. First Nations "began to emerge from

"irrelevance" to policy makers after the Second World War, and their emergence accelerated in the 1960s."[13] There were several reasons for this: "wartime experiences and post-war intellectual fashions made the racist bases of government Indian policy increasingly untenable."[14] There were economic and political reasons too. First Nations "occupied territories that the dominant society now realized contained valuable and needed resources. Inuit were in strategically important locations, and growing knowledge in the south of the appalling conditions that prevailed in many northern communities drew government attention to the Arctic regions."[15] And First Nations and Inuit "now had effective political bodies that put pressure on the political parties to modify policies."[16]

This summary of Miller's analysis is set out for reasons found in another of his contributions to our understanding of this subject: *Residential Schools and Reconciliation: Canada Confronts Its History.*[17] His thesis in that book is that a serious impediment to reconciliation is "the inability of Canadians to overcome their flawed, overly positive understanding of their country's history."[18] An understanding of history does not guarantee that we will learn from it, but without such understanding we cannot do so.

It is unimaginable that a "flawed, overly positive understanding" of our history persists to this day. Revelations that residential school sites include the graves of hundreds if not thousands of their captive pupils attest to the folly and brutality of attempting to forcefully assimilate Indigenous peoples into a non-Indigenous culture. Canadians have had their eyes opened to this dark chapter in their history.

As noted, the fourth phase of the relationship between Indigenous and non-Indigenous peoples is incomplete, and reconciliation – however it progresses – will be a central theme of the story. As of early 2020, the signs were not propitious. CN Rail's Eastern Canada operations and VIA's passenger service across the country were shut down after four hundred trains were cancelled because of Indigenous blockades of rail lines. There were blockades in Ontario, Quebec, and British Columbia, and other transportation routes were closed or compromised. The protests were in support of some of the hereditary chiefs of the clans of the Wet'suwet'en nation, who were opposed to the Coastal Gas-Link pipeline and who attracted sympathetic protests elsewhere, including among non-Indigenous supporters.[19]

The direct and indirect costs of the protests were massive. Weeks after they began, the *Globe and Mail*'s Matthew McClearn reported that "small businesses and manufacturing plants will be shuttered. Store shelves will go unstocked. Chicks will freeze to death in unheated barns. Canada's reputation among its trading partners will plummet."[20] Railway cars sat empty or carried lower volumes of freight. Grain producers were turned away from overflowing silos, whose contents were not transferred to waiting ships. Double the usual numbers of ships remained empty and anchored in Vancouver awaiting their cargo. On the Atlantic coast, the Port of Halifax lost an estimated 50 per cent of its volume as ships sailed instead to nearby American ports.[21] A poll in the wake of the protests found that 69 per cent of Canadians thought their country was broken.[22]

While these protests do not reflect unanimous opposition to the Coastal GasLink pipeline – elected chiefs support the project – they do represent a significant challenge to resolving differences: Indigenous communities are widely dispersed throughout the country and are without centralized leadership and policy. They are "a collection of widely differing interests, pressure groups, power points and varying regional, political and economic agendas that are often at odds across geographical regions, and within communities themselves."[23]

The protests do not mean, as some have claimed, that reconciliation is an empty promise or a stalled project. Recent decades have seen many legal decisions, commissions, policy changes, well-documented studies, and institutional initiatives – not least in our universities – aimed at improving the lives of Indigenous peoples. What is missing is a framework for reconciliation that marks a coherent path forward and sets out the implications for the Canadian state.

In *Indigenous Nationals, Canadian Citizens* (2018), Tom Courchene outlines three alternative models for developing this framework:

(1) Indigenous nationals/Indigenous citizens, (2) Indigenous nationals/Canadian citizens, and (3) Canadian nationals/Canadian citizens.[24] He argues that history has passed by the first and third, leaving the second as the compelling alternative. He views this as comparable to Quebecers within Canada; they are Quebec nationals and Canadian citizens. There is, however, an important difference: Quebecers are a geographically based collective with provincial status and a government that represents all of them, whereas Indigenous peoples occupy more than six hundred First Nations of variable capacities and speak fifty different languages; besides that, growing numbers across the country are moving from reserves to cities.

Courchene labels his model "the Commonwealth of Sovereign Indigenous Nations or CSIN."[25] It "could apply to a province or series of provinces ... or could even become a pan-Canadian model."[26] However, his illustration focuses on Saskatchewan because it has conditions in the present day that he considers relatively favourable to such a project. With seventy-four reserves, an overarching Federation of Sovereign Indigenous Nations (succeeding the Federation of Saskatchewan Indian Nations), and a strong institutional base, the context is already in place for evolution toward province-wide Indigenous governance with regional governments, including a public service charged with internal matters as well as relations with Ottawa and Regina. Status and Non-Status off-reserve Indigenous persons living in Saskatchewan would come under its jurisdiction.

Implementation would require major changes. "The fact that reserve land is a common property resource under the Indian Act is a huge deterrent to economic development on reserves,"[27] so a secure property rights regime would be required. "Also needed are an effective governance regime, an appropriate legal framework, and stable fiscal arrangements."[28] The latter would include revenue and expenditure measures commensurate with the creation of a new order of government with powers comparable to those of the provinces – possibly greater if the model were a pan-Canadian one. It must be said that the inclusion of off-reserve Indigenous persons within its jurisdiction is probably unworkable, and it is unlikely that the Government of Saskatchewan would welcome the province serving as a test case.

Courchene's proposal is one among several. A more nuanced conception is the one Alan Cairns laid out in *Citizens Plus: Aboriginal Peoples and the Canadian State* (2000).[29] Cairns contributed to the Hawthorn Report,[30] tabled more than three decades before his book, and so was among those who first recommended that "Indians should be regarded as 'citizens plus.' In addition to the normal rights and duties of citizenship, Indians possess certain additional rights as charter members of the Canadian community."[31] The words and the concept were subsequently voiced by Harold Cardinal, author of *The Unjust Society* (1999),[32] and by leading Indigenous organizations in Manitoba, Alberta, and British Columbia,[33] before they faded in the late 1970s and early 1980s. They had given way to Charter litigation and to legal scholarship that has verged on "monolithic in its focus on and support for self-governing Aboriginal nations. It displays minimal interest in Canadian citizenship, or in the more general question of what kind of overall Canadian community will coexist with Aboriginal self-government. What holds us together – why we should feel obligations to each other – is not on its agenda."[34] It *was* on Cairns's agenda, however, and "citizens plus" was the concept he saw as most compatible with a substantial and continuing relationship between Indigenous and non-Indigenous Canadians.

Cairns recognized that treaty lands and self-government had become the major themes animating this relationship. Sensitive to context, though, he recognized two realities that would have to be addressed in negotiations: first, the growing numbers – now a majority – of Indigenous people who live in our cities and whose lives are necessarily intertwined with those of their fellow urban dwellers. Second, to quote Peter H. Russell,

> even for those Aboriginal people who seek to recover and maintain a more autonomous condition, a very high degree of political and economic integration is inescapable. For the autonomy they seek is, of necessity, limited and conditional ... The self-governing communities they seek, in order to satisfy material expectations ... will need large

fiscal transfers from other orders of government especially in the early rebuilding stages. They cannot expect to receive this support and maintain beneficial political association with the larger society unless they participate in the governing institutions of that society as active citizens rather than abrasive foreigners.[35]

This point has been underscored by the growing numbers of Indigenous candidates in our recent elections: 54 candidates with 11 elected in 2015, 63 with 10 elected in 2019.[36] Unlike Quebec's Bloc members, they do not see themselves as temporary parliamentarians pending separation from Canada.

J.R. Miller concludes that recent decades have seen "modest progress toward reconciliation."[37] Churches "began to grapple with the legacy of residential schools in the 1980s and 1990s,"[38] and formal apologies followed. A revisionist history inspired by the Royal Commission on Aboriginal Peoples demonstrated that far from being "benevolent in intent and far-sighted in nature,"[39] "misguided" federal policies caused many of the social problems in Indigenous communities.[40] The $350 million Aboriginal Healing Foundation promoted "healing among individuals and communities that had been blighted by exposure to residential schools."[41] Prime Minister Stephen Harper apologized in the House of Commons in 2008 for the residential schools, and the following year, the Truth and Reconciliation Commission began to address their legacy, presenting a final report in 2015. The commission's report has been cited in aid of important initiatives to address this legacy. Initiatives "at the individual and local level ... have the potential to maintain the momentum behind the reconciliation movement,"[42] though Miller is cautious about the prospects of sweeping structural change along the way.

A new generation of scholars is grappling with the issues, and some of them would accept "profound destabilization,"[43] perhaps the end of Canadian federalism altogether, as an acceptable price for Indigenous self-determination. Canadians should understand that radical change is on the agenda and not only for those who man the blockades. Indigenous law issues are complex, as we know from Gordon Christie, who recently shared his personal quest to

understand them:[44] a "journey made difficult by labyrinthine jurisprudence presenting a deeply puzzling face and presence of strong
disagreement from observers as to what the law seems to express
and the nature of impacts it has had on lives and peoples."[45]

Christie's deep analysis defies summary, but we can outline
his thesis. The "colonial roots of Crown–Indigenous relations"[46]
remain unaddressed because of varying ideological perspectives
that have been generated by different sociocultural collectives,
whether those of Indigenous communities or non-Indigenous
ones in the larger Canadian society. The law of Indigenous rights
rests largely "on a bedrock of liberal thought, judges of the
Supreme Court building a new social structure out of architec-
tural principles grounded in a liberal vision of how society should
be ordered, with liberal ideals and values infusing the edifice then
erected."[47] But these may not be the values of Indigenous communities, some of which remain on the edges of mainstream legal
doctrine. The question that naturally follows is this: "Could contemporary liberalism be brought to a point where its adherents
might respond to insights into Indigenous self-determination?"[48]
Christie does not answer that question, but his thinking is that
"while the direction liberal thought tacks may be shifted, the ship
itself is fairly immune to radical change, and the general direction towards which the ship heads cannot be seriously altered.
Responding adequately to Indigenous self-determination would
be radical."[49]

Christie points to two camps in which scholars in the field
are clustered: "those who work (consciously or not) within
a normative world of liberal thought, and those who work to
maintain grounded forms of Indigenous self-determination."[50]
And, we might add, there are nuanced perspectives in between.
Aaron Mills, who is Anishinaabe from Couchiching First Nation
as well as a McGill University law professor, asserts that "self-
determination is the language of our settler colonizer":[51] "There's
no sovereignty for a rooted, growing, political community: sovereignty is a peoples-level articulation of an autonomous, not
a relational, conception of self. If we're always already connected in relations of deep interdependence, then the question

of freedom is never about standing apart from the other and always about how to stand with it."[52]

Mills draws our attention to his concept of rooted constitutionalism. He invites us to contemplate the image of a tree grounded in the earth by its roots, trunk extending upwards, branches of different shapes and sizes growing outward and supporting a canopy of leaves that flourish before falling and returning to earth, "and the circle continues."[53] There are different possibilities for the shape, size, and reach of the tree; similarly, healthy human societies "grow from, through and in"[54] the earth, or the stories we tell about it. The trunk is our constitutional order; the branches our legal traditions, the leaves our provisional norms.[55] "Once we see that we come from and return to the same place ... a good relationship is, at least, always possible."[56]

Mills is rooted in his First Nation and works within an institution (McGill University) grounded in Western culture and Enlightenment values. These are two different camps, and while he has a foot in both, he is not betwixt and between. The argument developed in his PhD thesis "isn't merely that Canadian constitutionalism has the effect of being colonial, but rather that as a principle actively applied in judicial reasoning, settler supremacy is part of the means of Canadian constitutionalism."[57] Furthermore, in arguing that "liberalism, rule of law and capitalism are settler forms of political, legal and economic ordering respectively, openly hostile to interdependence,"[58] he invites the inevitable question: if liberalism, rule of law, and capitalism are openly hostile to interdependence, is reconciliation only possible without them?

Glen Coulthard, author of *Red Skin, White Masks*,[59] offers an unambiguous answer to this question:

> The conceptions of reciprocity that inform many Indigenous peoples' understanding of land and relationship cannot be established with, or mediated through, the coercive institutions of state and capital. These constitutive features of Canada need to be radically transformed for an authentic relationship of peace, reciprocity and respect to take root. In order to build a truly decolonized set of relationships grounded in respect and reciprocity we need to sink the ship.[60]

Coulthard offers a stark choice. If an end to liberalism, the rule of law, and the market economy were a prerequisite for reconciliation, it would be an insurmountable barrier. As Christie suggests, state disavowal of these cannot be expected – indeed, it is impossible – in Canada. They are part of the architecture of this country and of other complex democratic states in the West. There will be differences about their meaning and reach, but short of revolution or populist takeover, they will remain the context for the unfolding story of the Canadian federation. They may bar reconciliation for those ideologically disposed to their end, but for the rest of us, the work must continue.

How should it continue? John Borrows tells us that Indigenous and non-Indigenous peoples must reconcile themselves with the earth,[61] and a focus on the sustainability of our common home offers a constructive framework for relationships. James Tully agrees, but adds that reconciliation with the earth is interconnected with "the reconciliation of Indigenous and non-Indigenous people (Natives and newcomers) with each other in all our diversity."[62] He recognizes "the enormity of the task of the two projects of reconciliation"[63] in that humans have become "conscripts of a vicious social system."[64] He does not despair in the face of its enormity: "Everyone can engage in practices of reconciliation here and now":[65]

> As the small, local, symbiotically coordinated webs of steps and practices of reconciliation grow, they first reach tipping points and bring about transformations of vicious relationships locally. These small changes have significant ripple effects ... If these continue to multiply and accumulate, here, there, and everywhere, they have the potential gradually to reach a point where the global vicious system as a whole is transformed into an assemblage of virtuous ones.[66]

We should not be diverted from Tully's important message by differences about whether local or global systems are "vicious," broken, or in disrepair. These differences are part of the varying ideological perspectives described by Christie. The importance of Tully's contribution is that it offers assurance that we can make a difference, individually – in small and informal collectives – and in larger, systemic ways. Tully does not discuss the "formal reconciliation procedures carried on by governments, courts and commissions; "[67] his topic is "the more basic, informal, and transformative practices of reconciliation and the shared responsibilities we all have"[68] to engage in them. But formal reconciliation remains on our agenda.

It is clear that we cannot take the definition of reconciliation as a given, agreed upon by all. Its common meaning is the restoration of good relations, but there aren't always past good relations to restore. This points to the wisdom of the approach offered by the Truth and Reconciliation Commission: "Reconciliation is about establishing and maintaining a mutually respectful relationship between Aboriginal and non-Aboriginal peoples in this country. In order for that to happen, there has to be awareness of the past, an acknowledgment of the harm that has been inflicted, atonement for the causes, and action to change behaviour."[69]

The main impediment to awareness – as J.R. Miller has written – has been the combination of myth and propaganda that supported a positive history of Canada's treatment of Indigenous peoples when the opposite was the case. Residential schools were the prime example of this "whitewashed" history,[70] and we have seen that its influence should have passed. Even before previously noted revelations of unmarked graves at residential school sites, a 2016 study conducted by the Environics Institute identified a growing awareness of Indigenous issues among non-Indigenous Canadians "and a widespread belief in the importance of moving forward to find meaningful solutions."[71] This study was completed only one year after the final report of the Truth and Reconciliation Commission, which has continued to receive positive attention in the years since it was tabled.

The second component of reconciliation – acknowledgment – was advanced in 2008 by Prime Minister Harper's "emotionally powerful speech of apology"[72] for residential schools in the House of Commons. Apologies matter, both for the state and for those to whom an apology is directed.

Regardless of whether they are aimed at image repair, therapy, or justice, all state apologies involve the construction of state identity in more than one way. First, in admitting responsibility for something done in the past, the state is making a claim about its unity, continuity, and sameness in time ... Second, in expressing its regret over its actions in the past, the state is also asserting its moral superiority over its past self.[73]

For those to whom the apology is offered, the words of the Truth and Reconciliation Commission are apposite.

Apologies are important to victims of violence and abuse. Apologies have the potential to restore human dignity and empower victims to decide whether they will accept an apology or forgive a perpetrator. Where there has been no apology, or one that victims believe tries to justify the behaviour of perpetrators and evade responsibility, reconciliation is difficult, if not impossible, to achieve.[74]

The apologies from Canada and the churches were, observed the Commission, "a necessary first step in the process of reconciliation."[75]

The 2020 blockades of rail lines and other transportation routes have been a setback. In a Nanos poll published in March 2020,[76] 73 per cent of respondents expressed disapproval of them. This is no surprise given the costs and disruption summarized earlier. Recalling the Oka confrontation in 1990 during which a Quebec Provincial Police officer was killed, many Canadians favoured restraint. Perhaps more troubling – and more enduring – in the wake of the blockades is that, as shown by the same Nanos poll, "Canadians are much more pessimistic about the potential for reconciliation with Indigenous peoples."[77]

This pessimism must be overcome so that the third component of reconciliation – redress – can continue. It should not depend upon major structural change in the Canadian federation; such change is either unlikely or a distant prospect. Step by step, as we learned from James Tully, worthy initiatives can multiply and cumulatively have a major impact, and we know from the Truth and Reconciliation Commission what some of the steps might be.

Calls to action that address the high number of Indigenous children in the care of the state, the health of Indigenous peoples, and the overrepresentation of Indigenous people in prisons and jails must receive urgent attention. Actions that address education are also vital. This is "the new buffalo," according to proclamations by Indigenous leaders and educational institutions. There has been impressive progress at the post-secondary level, and commitments to its continuance are in place at post-secondary institutions across the country. Similar commitments are needed in primary and secondary education, where, despite some improvement, we have not seen the same sort of progress. Policy-makers and those who serve them should prioritize improvement in participation and results for Indigenous students at all levels. This does not mean that all of the commission's calls to action on education should be implemented,[78] but it does mean that, for reconciliation, no priority should be higher than education.

The Truth and Reconciliation Commission also called upon "federal, provincial, territorial and municipal governments to fully adopt and implement the United Nations Declaration on the Rights of Indigenous Peoples as the framework for reconciliation."[79] Prime Minister Trudeau has promised to implement the declaration, and in this regard, the words of his government's leader in the Senate prior to the 2019 election were unequivocal: "I have been asked to formally announce ... that in the forthcoming election, the Liberal Party of Canada will campaign on a promise to implement, as government legislation, the UN Declaration on the Rights of Indigenous Peoples."[80] The Liberal government was successful in that election and subsequently acted on its promise.

As there is no consensus on what legislative implementation of UNDRIP would mean for Canada, its constitution, and its laws, some caution is required. Of particular interest in this respect is Article 32(2), which declares: "States should consult and cooperate in good faith with the Indigenous peoples concerned through their own representative institutions in order to obtain their free and informed consent prior to the approval of any project affecting their lands or territories and other resources, particularly in connection with the development, utilization or exploitation of mineral, water or other resources."

Issues of interpretation and process are embedded in this article, as was illustrated in the controversy over the Coastal GasLink pipeline project. When constructed, this natural gas pipeline will run 670 kilometres from Dawson Creek to the northwest BC coastal region. It was approved by the province and supported in writing by the band councils of twenty First Nations along the route, including those in the Wet'suwet'en territory. It was resisted, however, by the hereditary chiefs of the five clans that comprise that First Nation. The Wet'suwet'en blocked the only road accessing the pipeline construction. In December 2019 the British Columbia Supreme Court granted an injunction against the blockades and mandated the RCMP to enforce it.

Within a week, Wet'suwet'en hereditary chiefs issued an eviction notice to Coastal GasLink, demanding that the province cancel all work permits for the project and that the RCMP leave the territory. The chiefs cited a UN committee report urging that construction of the pipeline be ended because it did not have the free, prior, and informed consent of Indigenous peoples. They could have added that British Columbia has passed legislation implementing the UNDRIP.

Obvious questions follow. Is consultation in good faith by pipeline proponents sufficient, or do Indigenous peoples have an effective – though not a legal – veto over the project? Which Indigenous peoples must be consulted or have the capacity to halt the project? How are differences among them to be reconciled? Do the views of band councils carry more weight than those of hereditary chiefs? And if the hereditary chiefs' views hold sway, do only those opposed to the project count? What of the hereditary chiefs who *support* the pipeline, including three women who were stripped of their hereditary titles for supporting it?[81] Looming over these complex questions is the issue of the authority of Canadian jurisdictions, including British Columbia, to prescribe conditions for the approval of major resource projects, which, when met, will allow them to proceed.

As of this writing, work on the pipeline has resumed, though underlying governance issues remain unaddressed. Theresa Tait-Day, a founder of the Wet'suwet'en Matrilineal Coalition as well as one of the hereditary chiefs who was shorn of her title, explains: "By refusing to hear from elected councils [federal and provincial governments] have without merit prevented the most credible current governing voices from being heard ... The Indian Act system must be reformed, but that does not invalidate the role of the elected councils. While imperfect, they continue to speak for the people until a better model is implemented."[82]

Tait-Day's comment is supported by former justice minister Jody Wilson-Raybould's observation that the Wet'suwet'en must decide who speaks for them: "At its core the problem is really very simple. Who represents Indigenous peoples in Canada?"[83]

As Wilson-Raybould acknowledged, the problem is easier to state than it is to resolve, but the governance issues do not end here. In an article titled "Dysfunctional governance: Eleven Barriers to progress among Canada's First Nations,"[84] John Graham writes that the Indian Act is "widely (and rightly) criticized for its paternalism, among other things," but that it "is difficult to imagine repealing the act, given the lack of consensus on what might replace it."[85] He points to deteriorating or stalled numbers for many Indigenous communities in the Community Well-Being Index (CWB) and argues that dysfunction "is an important contributor."[86] He then turns his attention to the barriers. In point form and quoted verbatim, they are:

(1) First Nation governments are huge, perhaps the largest local governments in the world; (2) First Nations governments lack the array of checks and balances that governments in other parts of Canada face; (3) the number of politicians per capita knows no parallel in Canada and many are full-time and salaried; (4) there are a startling number of regulatory voids relating to land – environmental protection, natural resource management, construction standards and others; (5) First Nations are highly dependent on transfers from federal government departments and with very few exceptions generate no revenue from taxing their citizens or charging user fees; (6) the collective landholding system as set out in the Indian Act is a major brake on

economic development; (7) most First Nations communities are too small for efficient delivery of many of the services for which they have responsibility; (8) within First Nations, individuals have varying rights, a situation that promotes disunity and frustration; (9) the history of colonization has led to dependence and a strong sense of victimization for many First Nations; (10) First Nations and the federal and provincial governments have major differences on fundamental matters such as treaty and Aboriginal rights, fiduciary duties, and funding obligations; and (11) the federal government, the First Nations' most important "partner," is highly siloed, with little capacity for a differentiated whole-of-community approach to First Nation development.

Some of these barriers are well-known, others less so, but they all merit attention in a broad discussion of reconciliation. The quality of governance and public administration matters in all communities and at all levels, and the requirements of good governance – responsibility, accountability, and transparency – do not vary with cultural differences. These issues have been raised before. The First Nations Governance Act was introduced by the Chrétien government, and inherited by that of Paul Martin, but eventually was dropped when it encountered strong resistance from First Nations leaders. In 2013 the Harper government succeeded in passing the First Nations Financial Transparency Act, but its effect was short-lived: soon after taking office the Trudeau government announced that it would no longer enforce the legislation. The issues will not go away. Sound public administration requires settled decision-making processes that allow the business of the country to go on without disruptions that would damage the lives and livelihoods of Canadians, and the reconciliation process must include them on the agenda. If the requirements of good governance are not practised in Indigenous and non-Indigenous communities alike, reconciliation will remain an incomplete ambition.

Conclusion

While important to our history, the image of settler-colonizers is no longer apposite to the Canadian state. The settler-colonizers are dead, and most of their descendants are committed to reconciliation with Indigenous peoples. Both have been joined in Canada by millions unconnected to the country's past and seeking only to better their lives in a new land – a modern, liberal, democratic state that ranks highly among its peers and is enviable for its rights and freedoms.

The deliberate paralysis of a transportation system responsible for the daily movement of essential goods and millions of people cannot be abided by any state. The costs of the Canadian blockades were enormous and incalculable, yet those blockades were officially tolerated for weeks. It is not surprising that in their wake, most Canadians felt their country was broken, particularly when they were offered no reassurance that it would not happen again.

Reconciliation must not be set back as a result. There is growing awareness and official acknowledgment of the harms of the past. Important redress is under way, and Canadians in general favour its continuance and acceleration. Most will continue to see redress in terms compatible with Canadian federalism; some may not. There are threads of contemporary Indigenous scholarship that turn away from the prospect of a nation-building project by Indigenous and non-Indigenous citizens alike. This is not hostility to Canada so much as indifference to the country as a positive influence in Indigenous lives. That sentiment is not monolithic, but it is significant, and it will challenge all Canadians, including our national leaders, whose first duty is to preserve national unity. Fortunately, we are not faced with an either/or proposition: the status quo or radical change. As Greg Poelzer and Ken Coates observe, "the rejection of extreme positions on both sides of the debate still leaves an enormous amount of space for innovation, creativity and new ideas."[87] We must continue to explore that space in the interests of both Indigenous self-determination and Canadian citizenship.

chapter four

Immigrants, Migration, and Citizenship

"We are all immigrants" is a common truism among those who would remind others of the importance of newcomers[1] in the stories of their countries. In Canada we acknowledge that some of us are indigenous to these lands, but for newcomers those words serve as an invocation of equal citizenship for all who came and stayed here.

Immigrants are "persons residing in Canada who were born outside Canada, excluding temporary foreign workers, Canadian citizens born outside Canada, and those with student or working visas."[2] Refugees are persons "who have been forced to leave their country in order to escape war, persecution or natural disaster."[3] Migrants are persons who move "from one place to another, especially in order to find work or better living conditions."[4]

Welcoming more immigrants to Canada has been a policy of successive governments. The present one extols "modest and responsible increases ... with a focus on welcoming highly skilled people who can help build a stronger Canada."[5] When distinguished from arrivals by refugees and migrants, immigration is a comparatively orderly and predictable process. That said, when immigrants, refugees, and migrants are viewed generically as newcomers, common themes emerge.

The University of Toronto's Joseph Carens does not accept what he calls the conventional view that "every country has the right to decide who gets in and who doesn't."[6] He supports open borders as an expression "of human moral equality and freedom,"[7] and he envisions "a global order in which people are free to stay at home or move as they choose."[8] He does not anticipate hundreds of millions of people on the move, because, if their living conditions are adequate, most people will choose to remain in their familiar surroundings with family and friends nearby. The proviso – *if their living conditions are adequate* – is important here, because Carens argues that "restrictions on immigration are ultimately a way of protecting privilege."[9] His analogy is feudalism: "Those of us who live in the rich countries of Europe and North America are like the nobility and the vast majority of people in the world who live elsewhere are poor and impoverished like the peasants."[10] The former have a moral obligation to uplift the latter: "We should change the terms of trade. We should provide development aid. We should change the rules of the international system so that countries are not so disadvantaged."[11]

Carens is not alone in his support for open borders,[12] and if his view prevailed, the distinction between immigrants, refugees, and migrants would fade. But while there may be regional or continental easing of cross-border movement – the European Community is an example – open borders are not coming soon if at all. Nation-states are this world's principal subdivisions, and their governments are charged with public administration of their affairs, including the regulation and oversight of newcomers. These states view a capacity to control numbers as an element of their sovereignty, as well as necessary in that they must provide infrastructure and services for new arrivals, address any security issues they may present, and help them integrate into their new country. And in democratic states they must do so with the tolerance if not support of their populations.

And so we return to immigrants, refugees, and migrants. A 2019 national poll conducted by the Environics Institute found that Canadians are *not* becoming less receptive to the more than 300,000 newcomers who arrive each year. Overall, "there is no public consensus on the impact of immigrants and refugees, with significant segments of the population holding opposing views. But as has been the case most of the past two decades, positive sentiments outweigh negative ones on such questions as the overall level of immigration, its positive impact on the economy, its low impact on crime rates, and the impact on the country as a whole."[13]

The same poll disclosed that while immigrants and refugees were not top of mind among the concerns of Canadians in 2019, there were differences of opinion on the subject that were a function of on age, education, and residence: "Positive sentiments are most prevalent among younger Canadians, immigrants and people with a university education. Negative views are most evident in Alberta, among Canadians ages 60 and older, and those without a high school diploma."[14] But whether pro or con, most Canadians – 80 per cent – agree that Canada is a welcoming country for both immigrants and refugees.[15]

Polls later in 2019 posted different results. A poll commissioned by the CBC found that 64 per cent of Canadians were concerned about illegal immigration;[16] a Léger poll recorded 63 per cent favouring stronger limits on immigration;[17] and an Ipsos poll saw 54 per cent reporting Canada to be too welcoming to immigrants.[18] "Experts say the findings are not surprising in that there is a general shift in many countries around the world against migrants and immigration."[19] In Canada, they said, this attitude shift was not helped by the tens of thousands of people who walked across the US border into Canada to claim asylum following a tweet by the prime minister in 2017.[20] In apparent response to a US ban on travellers from seven Muslim-majority countries, he had tweeted: "To those fleeing persecution, terror & war, Canadians will welcome you, regardless of your faith. Diversity is our strength #Welcome to Canada." The ensuing spike in asylum-seekers and illegal entrants provoked a backlash, reflected in the polling numbers, that did not distinguish among immigrants, refugees, and migrants.

The backlash may have been aggravated by misinformation. An Angus Reid poll published in late 2019 revealed that most Canadians do not know the countries from which most immigrants come (South and Southeast Asia) or the proportion that are refugees (15%) or the number that come as economic immigrants rather than as refugees or through family reunification.[21] Social media may be partly the reason: "Because immigration is a well-established topic for communication and because it is particularly concerning to a lot of people, it is a very useful lever to pull when spreading disinformation."[22]

Whatever the reasons, the prime minister's tweet was a reminder that Canadians expect newcomers to be welcomed and supported through established processes that are difficult to circumvent and understandable to the general public. Sentiment toward immigration may well vary depending on current exigencies, but there is no reason to believe that the attitudes reported by Environics have shifted permanently or for long. As long as they trust the process, Canadians will continue to welcome immigrants and the talents and cultural richness they bring to the country.

This observation is supported by the work of Allison Harell of the University of Quebec at Montreal and her colleagues at McGill and Stanford.[23] Based on online surveys of more than two thousand Americans and Canadians, one that included vignettes about individual immigrants' circumstances, including their photographs, these scholars concluded that "economic factors make a significant difference in citizens' evaluation of potential immigrants in both the U.S. and Canada."[24] Furthermore, "if ethnicity and skin matter for citizens' evaluation of individual immigrants, they appear to do so only to a small degree."[25] In Canada, "there are not clear differences in support across either ethnicity or complexion."[26] This survey, together with comparative literature, suggests that "Canadians tend to be, relatively speaking, tolerant of both immigration and ethnic diversity." Harell and her colleagues also conclude that "high levels of support for immigration in Canada is bolstered by a comparatively selective Canadian system."[27]

To this point the discussion has not taken into account two wider trends to which we now turn: global population growth, and migration. The world's population has grown from one billion people in 1800 to nearly eight billion today, and the UN Department of Economic and Social Affairs expects it to reach nearly ten billion by the middle of this century and more than eleven billion by 2100[28] (this estimate was revised downward to 10.9 billion in 2019). Growth is uneven around the globe. Today about two thirds of earth's population live in Africa or Asia; by 2100 it will be four fifths. Africa will be the fastest-growing region until 2050. Half of world population growth will occur in only nine countries, and the United States is the only high-income country on that list.[29]

If the UN forecast is sound, we can anticipate that an additional four billion people will bring food supply and other pressures to bear on the planet and that the pressures will be greatest on countries less able to endure them. But not everyone agrees with these numbers. In their book *Empty Planet*,[30] John Ibbitson and Darrell Bricker argue that by the middle of this century the global population will begin a consistent decline with no end in sight: "an increasing number of demographers around the world believe the UN estimates are far too high. More likely, they say, the planet's population will peak at around nine billion sometime between 2040 and 2060, and then start to decline."[31] A smaller population will bring some benefits, but, the authors warn, "enormous disruption lies ahead, too. We can already see the effects in Europe and parts of Asia, as aging populations and worker shortages weaken the economy and impose crippling demands on healthcare and social security."[32] And if Richard Saillant is prescient, we will be seeing the effects soon in Canada too, particularly in the eastern provinces.[33]

The point here is that population growth may not be the destabilizing force it is widely feared to be. But even on the Ibbitson–Bricker projections, over at least the next three decades we will be encountering questions about our responsibilities as more than a billion people are added to the earth's numbers. Canada is the second-largest country in the world by area, and among the least densely populated, so we will be looked upon as a country that can accommodate more immigrants and refugees. We may even need to accommodate more if Ibbitson, Bricker, and Saillant are all correct. Declining numbers in the workforce, particularly in eastern Canada, will challenge the social programs we have put in place to support the population as a whole. On either scenario – population growth or population decline – immigration will continue to be an important topic of conversation. We must have immigration policies that transcend partisan political differences and that are broadly acceptable to Canadians, and we need a continuing and mature debate on what those policies should be.

Regarding migration, its history actually predates *Homo sapiens*, and the reasons our ancestors had for migration resonate to this day. "Where for some groups a change in climate may have pushed them to seek more hospitable lands, others may have been looking for better food sources, avoiding hostile or competing neighbours or may have simply been curious risk-takers wanting a change of scenery."[34] Today, in addition to regional hostilities and other local concerns, geopolitical issues including climate change may soon drive migration on a greater scale than we have witnessed to date.

Migrants may also be refugee claimants or immigrants, but how they present themselves matters and affects how their cases are determined. Elderly Canadians may remember one of our more recent experiences with migration. In May 1939 a passenger ship sailed from Nazi Germany, destined for Cuba, with more than nine hundred Jews on board, most of them former German citizens whose citizenship had been revoked in 1935 by Hitler's Nuremberg Laws. The MS *St. Louis* arrived in Havana two weeks later; after unsuccessful attempts over several days to land its passengers, it was ordered to leave Cuban waters. It sailed along the US coast while Americans pro and con debated whether the passengers should be allowed to disembark and join the ranks of asylum-seekers. Concerned about the domestic impact of violating quota limits and admitting the *St. Louis* passengers ahead of others on the waiting list,[35] President Roosevelt said no, and the ship sailed north toward Halifax while Canadians also debated their fate. Our government, too, said no, and the ship returned to Europe to disembark its passengers, many of whom later died as the Holocaust spread across the continent.[36]

The historical record reveals that some of the Canadian resistance was rooted in fears of mass migration. In the words of Frederick Blair, then director of Canada's Immigration Branch, "no country ... could open its doors wide enough to take in the hundreds of thousands of Jewish people who want to leave Europe: the line must be drawn somewhere."[37] That it was drawn to exclude fewer than a thousand migrants stranded on the ocean and in foreseeable peril if entry was refused was a tragic decision for which the country apologized nearly eighty years later.

In contrast to the *St. Louis* episode, the story of the migrant (and inaccurately named) "boat people" was, for Canada, a positive one. A refugee crisis in Southeast Asia in the aftermath of the Vietnam War and regime changes in Cambodia and Laos saw about three million refugees on the move by land, sea, and air. Canada had by then become more hospitable to refugees, with nearly forty thousand Hungarians admitted after the 1956 uprising in their country was crushed by the Soviet Union, and with the signing in 1969 of the UN Convention Relating to the Status of Refugees. In the 1970s and 80s about two hundred thousand Vietnamese, Cambodians, and Laotians were resettled in Canada – "the highest rate per capita among all of the countries that have accepted such refugees."[38] For their hospitable response to the refugee crisis, Canadians were awarded the UN Nansen Medal in 1986 "in recognition of major and sustained efforts made on behalf of refugees."[39] It is the only occasion since the medal's inception in 1954 that it was awarded to an entire population.[40]

Canada continues to welcome refugees – including twenty-five thousand from war-torn Syria in 2015–16 – though we should not expect an end to the controversy that sometimes accompanies them. We have seen that immigration issues in general are exploitable for reasons that often play on insecurity, a phenomenon not limited to Canada. When a leading international newsmagazine, *The Economist*, published a special report on migration in 2019, the editors anticipated that their argument that the world needs more migration might be unpopular.[41] They were aware of the fears underlying the topic, so they countered with what they called The Magic of Migration.[42]

The magic is that increased migration would make the world wealthier, potentially twice as wealthy if all who wanted to migrate could do so. "No other policy change comes close to generating such colossal rewards":[43] "Migrants who move from lower- to higher-income countries typically earn three to six times more than they did at home, according to the World Bank. The simple act of moving makes them more productive, because rich countries have better institutions, the rule of law, efficient capital markets and modern companies."[44]

Two thirds of skilled migrants move to four countries: America, Britain, Canada, and Australia. "All four are rich, English-speaking and have top-notch universities – a crucial draw. Three were founded on the notion that immigrants could go there and create a new life; the other, Britain, has a long tradition ... of cosmopolitan tolerance."[45]

Is the magic of migration the poaching of talent by rich countries from poor ones? Is one country's brain gain another's brain drain? *The Economist* contends that this argument is too simplistic.[46] Migrants send money back to their home countries – their remittances are three times greater than foreign aid.[47] They stay in touch with them and sometimes return to start businesses; and even the prospect of migration to richer countries "changes the incentives for people in poor countries. It prompts more of them to get educated and acquire marketable skills. Having acquired these skills, many who intended to emigrate never do ... Many who do emigrate, ultimately return."[48]

There are other popular concerns, most of them unfounded: migrants are a drain on the welfare state (only if the host state makes it too easy to draw benefits or too hard to work); migrants steal jobs from locals (they add jobs, too, with the additional economic activity they represent); too many migrants "leads to overcrowding, congestion, high house prices and environmental stress."[49] Better urban development policies can address the first three of these, and the "impact of migration on climate change is probably small."[50] Migrants may emit more carbon than they did at home, but "migration causes fertility to plunge ... Ethnic Somali women have an average of 6.2 kids in Somalia but only 2.4 in Norway."[51]

There remain two concerns of greater substance. The first is that migrants, particularly Muslims, will bring with them beliefs or behaviours from their native countries that may undermine democratic civil societies in their host countries; the second is that population growth combined with climate change may see widespread migration on a scale heretofore unimagined. Historian Niall Ferguson raised the spectre of the former when, after ruing the history of the twentieth century, he wrote:

A century ago it was the west's great blunder to think it would not matter if Lenin and his confederates took over the Russian Empire, despite their stated intention to plot world revolution and overthrow both democracy and capitalism. Incredible as it may seem, I believe we are capable of repeating that catastrophic error. I fear that, one day, we shall wake with a start to discover that the Islamists have repeated the Bolshevik achievement, which was to acquire the resources and capability to threaten our existence.[52]

Ferguson may have in mind Al-Qaeda, Afghanistan's Taliban, and Islamic State of Iraq and the Levant (ISIL) – Islamist organizations that have been internationally condemned for terrorism and violations of international human rights standards. In responding to the fear that migrant Muslims might undermine Western democratic states, we should bear in mind the distinctions made by Akbar Ahme, Chair of Islamic Studies at American University:

I see three broad, sometimes overlapping, categories within Islam: literalist Islam – those Muslims who believe that to be a good Muslim should mean to adhere to the letter and spirit of Islamic law; the mystics – those who believe in a warm, inclusive embrace of humanity which reflects the love of the divine for all creation; and finally the modernists – those who believe in balancing faith with modernity. Those in this final category believed that modernity, with its characteristics of democracy and accountability, and Islam were compatible. It is this category that is under direct threat from the literalists.[53]

Muslim legal scholar Abdullahi Ahmed An-Na-im is clearly in the modernist category. He writes: "The Shari'a law of apostasy can easily be abused and has been abused in the past to suppress political opposition and inhibit spiritual and intellectual growth."[54] In *Toward an Islamic Reformation* (1990), he argues for the "reform of the historical formulations of Islamic law."[55]

Literalist adherence to the letter and spirit of unreformed Islamic law, and rejection of the separation of church (mosque) and state, are incompatible with public life in Canada. When literalist or other extremist voices are heard in our midst (for example, an Imam preaching in Montreal reportedly incited violence against Jews, and a Toronto Imam is said to have proposed death for gay men), they should be prosecuted for hate speech. When fundamentalists urge women to accept patriarchy and remain in their homes except when they must go out, they should publicly be held accountable for violating equality standards and values in Canada.[56] But we should not be preoccupied by literalist or other extremist voices. In general, Muslims in Canada are modernists and live peacefully among their fellow Canadians as neighbours and friends.

There remains the second big concern noted earlier: population growth combined with climate change may see widespread migration on a scale heretofore unimagined. There are sharply different views on this subject, and our purpose is not to choose from among them; rather, it is to weigh the consequences of each for the choices implicit in our narrative.

We begin with the link between overpopulation and climate change. Canadians Pierre Desrochers and Joanna Szurmak have reviewed the work of both optimists and pessimists on the subject and place themselves among the optimists.[57] Our current numbers reflect a success story: "humans are now taller, stronger and healthier than ever before" and have almost doubled their life expectancies over three centuries. The authors cite economist Julian Simon, who describes the rapid rise in life expectancy as "the greatest single achievement in history."[58] They make their case "for both population growth and fossil fuel-powered economic development as the only practical way, now and in the near future, to lift much of humanity out of poverty, to build resilience against any downsides of increased anthropogenic greenhouse gas emissions, and to make possible a sustained reduction of humanity's impact on its environment."[59]

Desrochers and Szurmak find some support in the literature. "The claim that population growth, especially in the poorest countries, is a primary driver of climate change must be treated with major scepticism," according to a joint UN–UK publication.[60] But many voices assert the opposite. In 2014 the Intergovernmental Panel on Climate Change claimed that globally, "economic and population growth continued to be the most important drivers of increases in CO2 emissions from fossil fuel combustion."[61] And in late 2019, thousands of experts signed an emergency declaration that population decline is needed to address climate change.[62]

Climate change is going to lead to more migration: 140 million, according to the World Bank in 2018;[63] up to one billion migrants in the next forty years, according to the World Economic Forum.[64] Predictions are imprecise but all the numbers are high, and preferred destinations will include Europe and North America. The message to all of us is clear: prepare now.

Conclusion

In the previous chapter and this one, we have seen that newcomers have always been part of the history of Canada as we know it. In the colonial era, newcomers were our non-Indigenous ancestors, who were initially welcomed to North America by its Indigenous peoples. As the early centuries passed, they came in ever-larger numbers, in due course outnumbering and overwhelming their Indigenous hosts, who were eventually mistreated and sidetracked and who were excluded from Canadian citizenship until the mid-twentieth century. It may be that some contemporary resistance to newcomers is rooted in acknowledgment of what early Canadians did to Indigenous peoples, and anxiety about newcomers arriving in large numbers, perhaps changing our surroundings and lives in ways we can neither anticipate nor appreciate.

This is not our recent experience. The original French and British newcomers were joined by generations of others from all parts of the world, leading to the cosmopolitan country we have today. It is difficult to imagine what our recent past would have been had we closed our borders, built walls, and excluded newcomers, but we know we would be smaller in numbers, poorer, and more parochial. But we did not do those things; indeed, we committed ourselves to reconciliation with the original inhabitants of this land, thereby evolving in ways that ensure that newcomers continue to be welcome in Canada, as they should be.

Welcoming attitudes are not constant, however. They fluctuate and sometimes retrench and so must be encouraged and renewed. We have learned from Allison Harell and others that confidence in the processes underlying the numbers of newcomers identified and their admission into Canada is critical to sustaining support for welcoming them.

Migration stirs unease, and sometimes hostility, because it is unpredictable and sometimes chaotic and because it inspires fears of a future in which there will be mass migration resulting from wars, dysfunctional or corrupt governments, population growth, and climate change. To date migrants have largely changed locations in their own countries or overflowed into neighbouring or proximate ones. But the prospect of global migration caused by climate change, and in numbers that will challenge the capacities of host states to receive them, is becoming more immediate. That will require the international community to monitor, anticipate, and plan for that eventuality, and it will require each potential host country to determine where it stands on the global landscape to come.

chapter five

Economic Opportunity and Citizenship

Aristotle might have agreed with Prime Minister Trudeau's decision to create a new cabinet portfolio for middle-class prosperity; he believed that societies ruled by a middle class were more just and stable than others. There is no agreement on definitions or on what makes Canada different from less advantaged countries, but a majority of Canadians believe they are among the middle class of a quite prosperous country. That is conducive to the attachment of citizenship.

The security of that attachment is another matter. It depends on this country's continuing viability, which means, in a large decentralized federation like Canada, on integration of the parts (provinces and regions) with one another so as to form a whole. There is another factor to consider here, one that rose to prominence in early 2020 as the coronavirus spread around the world accompanied by the second global financial crisis in just over a decade. True, there are differences between those two crises: "the 2007–2009 crisis came from within the financial system,"[1] while the one in 2020 has been the consequence of a global health crisis. But their proximity in time, and their wide and severe impacts, lead us to reflect on the relationship between global and local economies and between global and Canadian citizenship.

We will concern ourselves here with our national economy, including its global context, and with the interactions of provincial and regional economies with one another and with Ottawa. Public opinion on those interactions will reflect different politics, ideologies, and perspectives. That said, there are also variables that cannot be ignored: comparisons with peers, competitiveness, productivity, business investment, innovation, growth, and the impact of all these on employment.

We begin with comparisons, two in particular – the G7 and the Organisation for Economic Co-operation and Development (OECD). Since 2017 Canada has fared well in comparisons of annual growth among G7 economies; it has been either in the lead or behind only the United States.[2] Among the larger group of OECD nations, Canada has also fared well in the eleven factors assessed for the OECD Better Life Index.[3] Our relative good fortune continues to register in these and other snapshots of our national life.

Snapshots capture moments in time, but it is underlying trends that reveal the moving picture. Consider, first, our competitiveness. In late 2019, Deloitte's Competitiveness Scorecard for the Business Council of Canada outlined Canada's strengths and weaknesses. The former included human talent, macroeconomic policy, and access to markets at home and abroad; among the latter were labour and skill shortages; fiscal deficits of both federal and provincial governments that limit their capacity to support the economy during downturns; the accumulation of household debt; underinvestment in public infrastructure; a lag in innovation; tax uncompetitiveness; and an outdated, cumbersome regulatory environment.[4] In the World Economic Forum's Global Competitiveness Report (2019), Canada ranked fourteenth and was on a three-year downward trajectory, well behind the United States (our most important trading partner), which placed second.

Lagging productivity continues to undermine the Canadian economy and is a particular concern in the country's most advanced industrial sectors.[5] In 2017 it was reported that "overall business investment in the economy remains weak"[6] and that the country stood sixteenth among the seventeen countries ranked for business investment as a share of GDP.[7]

Innovation continues to lag as well: "The reality in the knowledge-driven global economy is that the ownership of intellectual property (IP) is paramount and a precondition to commercialization.

Those who generate, own and commercialize valuable ideas have the greatest ability to create wealth. The rest – those companies and countries without deep IP stocks – will fight over table scraps."[8]

The past fifteen years have seen many reports documenting Canadian weakness in developing and exploiting intellectual property. TD Senior Economist Leslie Preston recently wrote that "Canada has persistently lagged the U.S. in IPP investment but the situation has been worsening. The U.S.'s dominance in the tech sector does not tell the whole story. Canada lags in most sectors, placing future productivity and a higher standard of living at risk."[9]

Citing weak business investment ($50 billion below 2014 levels) and other factors, the Conference Board of Canada projects growth averaging 1.7 per cent per year between 2020 and 2040.[10] This is not the end of growth predicted by some,[11] but long-term tepid growth in the production of goods and services (the gross domestic product) is mediocre economic performance at best.

What does all of this have to do with citizenship? Two things. First, while Canada fares well in current annual G7 and OECD indices, underlying trends point to weakening economic performance with diminishing opportunities for our citizens – not just in the short term but possibly for years to come. Second, while a vibrant, resilient economy may overshadow interprovincial and regional tensions within Canada, weakening economic performance may aggravate them. We turn now to that subject.

In *A Tale of Two Countries: How the Great Demographic Imbalance Is Pulling Canada Apart*,[12] the University of Moncton's Richard Saillant presents a demographic analysis that he argues points to a threat to Canada's national unity. Canada's population is aging overall, but its provinces are doing so at "vastly different speeds."[13] The divide is at the Ottawa River, with the eastern provinces aging more rapidly than those in the west. With slowing or declining participation in the workforce comes slower growth along with higher costs for providing services to seniors. The trend and its effects were modest in their early stages, but "the benign days of population aging are now behind us. And while it will affect the entire country in the years ahead, population aging will impact eastern provinces most, exerting severe pressures on their already strained public purses and dragging down their economic growth further than in the rest of the country."[14]

Saillant acknowledges that he is offering only a projection and that the demographic imbalance may change or moderate, but he thinks not. He offers "three related reasons why Canada's demographic imbalance will remain with us for at least the next quarter century":[15] birth rates are higher in younger, more westerly regions; migration will flow unevenly and more toward the west because newcomers "are more likely to concentrate in places that have already welcomed more migrants and are more dynamic economically – Vancouver and Toronto in particular";[16] and third, fertility rates are lower in the older east than in the younger west.

Saillant does not foresee developments that would alter his projection,[17] so we are left with the consequences: "Ultimately the fate of poorer provinces is in the hands of their richer counterparts. The centre of gravity of Canadian politics sits firmly in the lands west of the Ottawa River and will only move further west as time passes. The richer provinces, where the great majority of people live, will decide whether or not Canada's welfare state will tell a tale of two countries."[18]

Regional disparity in Canada is not new; the difference in 2020 is that weakening economic prospects for the country as a whole, exacerbated by new and old regional grievances, make it more difficult to address the problem.

We begin with equalization, in the amount of $19 billion in 2018–19. It is funded from general revenues in federal budgets, though we should remind ourselves that the money does not come from Ottawa or the provinces; it comes from the pockets and purses of Canadian taxpayers, who, broadly, should understand why and how their money is spent. The principle of equalization (not the formula) is protected by the Charter,[19] and its purpose is clear enough, and uncontroversial. It is intended "to reduce the differences in revenue-generating capacity across Canada's 10 provinces. By compensating poorer provinces for their relatively weak tax bases or resource endowments, equalization helps to ensure that Canadians residing in provinces have access to a reasonably similar level of provincial government services at reasonably similar levels of taxation, regardless of which province they call home."[20]

Yet fifty years after the program was established in 1957, a leading Canadian economist observed that it "lay in shambles."[21] The reasons are explored elsewhere, but we can note here that their legacy has been unfortunate language about haves and have-nots, confusion about how the program operates, mistrust of Ottawa by some provincial governments regarding the treatment of energy in the formula, and scepticism about the program's impact and future.

The formula has been changed by Liberal and Conservative governments alike, but complaints continue. In 2018 five scholars came together to offer their assessment of the program,[22] and two of their criticisms are noteworthy. First, "there is an increasing discrepancy between the size of the equalization pool and the size of the fiscal disparities among the provinces."[23] They argue that "the fiscal capacity of non-receiving provinces has shrunk while that of receiving provinces has increased,"[24] yet the size of the pool is not proportionately adjusted to reflect that change. Second, "fiscal capacity alone provides an incomplete picture of the ability of a province to provide public services and that expenditure needs (due to differences in demographics and costs of providing services) should also be taken into consideration."[25]

These scholars also propose a major change: "the fact that the federal government alone manages equalization means there is always the potential for politics to influence decisions about the program."[26] They encourage the federal government to set up "an arm's-length agency to determine payments and make recommendations for adjustments to the formula,"[27] citing Australia as an example. In that country, equalization is administered by the Commonwealth Grants Commission,

> an independent statutory body with members appointed by the federal government that makes recommendations in consultation with the federal government and the states. The commission aims to identify, and then quantify, those factors outside the control of the states that

affect their expenditure requirements and revenue-raising capacity, as opposed to their actual expenditure and revenue or fiscal position. It is this assessment of both expenditure needs and revenue-raising capacity that makes the Australia approach to fiscal equalization internationally unique in its comprehensiveness.[28]

The Australian process "equalises fiscal capacity, not fiscal outcomes. It also tries to avoid distorting decision-making by the states and the creation of perverse incentives to manipulate the system to obtain a larger grant share."[29]

Equalization is an essential feature of federalism in Canada – as it is of other federal states, such as Australia, Germany, Switzerland, and the United States – but "very little attention" has been given to the ways in which other federalist countries manage similar programs.[30] Our program is complicated, lacking in transparency, and increasingly contentious among provinces as well as between them and Ottawa. This points to a need for reform, and an examination of best practices in other federal states would be a good place to start.

While we are on the topic of reform, we might look to another inter-jurisdictional domain that needs attention: trade and commerce. The pursuit of international free trade agreements has been a high priority of recent federal governments, in notable contrast to our failure to create free trade at home within Canada. In 1994, the Agreement on Internal Trade committed the federal and provincial governments to tackling this problem. Yet twenty-two years later, in 2016, the Senate Committee on Banking, Trade and Commerce issued a report, evocatively titled "Tear Down These Walls: Dismantling Canada's Internal Trade Barriers," in which it lamented the lack of progress on this file and estimated the cost to the GDP at somewhere between $50 billion to $130 billion.[31]

It was not supposed to be this way. Section 121 of the Constitution Act, 1867, states: "All Articles of the Growth, Produce or Manufacture of any one of the Provinces shall, from and after the Union, be admitted free into each of the other provinces." On a literal reading the section is clear – free means free – but it has not been so interpreted. In what is popularly described as the free-the-beer case, Gerard Comeau drove in 2012 from his home in northeastern New Brunswick across the interprovincial boundary with Quebec and purchased beer and liquor for personal use. On his way home he was stopped by the RCMP, his purchase was confiscated, and he was charged under provincial legislation that makes it illegal to buy and transport more than a dozen pints of beer from another province to New Brunswick. Comeau contested the charge on the basis that it violated Section 121 – successfully at trial and when the New Brunswick Court of Appeal refused to entertain a prosecution appeal – but in 2018 the Supreme Court of Canada ruled against him in holding that the objective of New Brunswick's Liquor Control Act was to enable supervision of the production, movement, sale, and use of alcohol within the province and not to restrict interprovincial trade.[32]

This case illustrates the quandary that has impeded interprovincial free trade from the beginning: tariff barriers on internal trade within Canada are impermissible, but non-tariff barriers are not, and the latter are many and formidable. From protectionist measures related to shipping alcohol, to supply management in dairy products, to local preference in procurement policies and practices, and to myriad regulatory regimes, non-tariff barriers have frustrated internal free trade for most of our history. As the University of Calgary's Trevor Tombe observed in 2017, "countless thousands of sometimes small differences between provincial rules, regulations, certifications, standards, registration requirements, and so on, makes doing business across Canada difficult. This raises prices, lowers productivity and lowers income – all to the detriment of Canadian consumers and businesses."[33]

The Canadian Free Trade Agreement concluded in 2017 may change this, though its title promises more than it delivers. It is a framework agreement – a commitment to talk further, to address differences, and to negotiate. Tombe is among the optimists on its potential, though with a caution: the agreement "shouldn't be evaluated on what it will do on Day 1, but on the path it has set us on."[34] Still, with 135 pages of exemptions from the deal, minor penalties for infractions, and the heavy lifting ahead relegated to various working groups and side tables,[35] we should not hold our breath.

In summary, economic opportunities with marked variation by region or province can undermine the solidarity of citizenship. So too can internal trade restrictions that make it easier for foreign interests to do business in Canada than domestic ones. Globalization adds to the challenges. For many years Canada has made globalization through free trade agreements a national priority, and it now has them with all G7 partners and with more than fifty countries in total. Opinion on the merits is not unanimous. Celebrants point to recognized advantages of expanding markets; critics worry about negative consequences for income, employment, workplace conditions, and social supports and about the diminished state capacity to address them. It is acknowledged that there are winners and losers in the advancement of open markets, which may attenuate attachments by citizens to their home countries. While they do not lead inevitably to global citizenship, they do lead to a more global citizenship as goods, services, and people move more freely around the world with the shifting attachments that come with greater interdependence.

It may be that we will look back on early 2020 as a pre/post COVID-19 divide in international trade. On 2 April of that year, in the immediate wake of approval for the new NAFTA agreement, President Trump asked 3M to halt exports of its N95 face masks to Canada. 3M replied that stopping "all exports of respirators produced in the United States would likely cause other countries to do the same, as some have already done. If that were to occur, the net number of respirators being made available to the United States, would actually decrease. That is the opposite of what we and the administration ... both seek."[36]

The reassertion of protectionism will not be limited to respirators. While the 2008–9 financial crisis brought a major shock to world trade, "the shock coming this year threatens to be far more brutal. When one of the world's economic giants sneezes, the rest of the world catches cold. Now everyone is coughing. Factory closures are being exacerbated by a rise in trade barriers. And global demand is plummeting as households' incomes dry up and cash-strapped firms put their investment plans on ice."[37]

And trade barriers are going up. From restricted exports of medical supplies, to the crushing of tourism, to flight cancellations and the rising costs of shipments by air,[38] the decline of trade will be severe: "The pandemic-induced slowdown in consumer spending and investment is already becoming clear. And it has already dented trade activity badly."[39] Experts predict a drop much bigger than in 2008–9:[40] "A lesson from 2009 is that trade bounces back ... Trade thrives on trust and predictability. Today, with supply chains buckling and borders closing, both are in short supply."[41]

Conclusion

We should be concerned about the juxtaposition of Richard Saillant's analysis and the current issues with equalization. If his demographic analysis holds true, it will bring a new round of pressures on equalization or lead to other calls for redistribution when the federation is not well-equipped to shoulder them. We could make a further observation about the dimming prospects for advancing interprovincial trade as we enter a time of unknown severity and duration. Anticipating the financial consequences of the coronavirus, Bob Rae and Mel Cappe observed that "Canadians are facing the most serious economic and social crisis since the end of the Second World War."[42] Three senior leaders in the Boston Consulting Group state the problem facing all economies: "As the coronavirus continues its march around the world, governments have turned to proven public health measures, such as social distancing, to physically disrupt the contagion. Yet, doing so has severed the flow of goods and people, stalled economies, and is in the process of delivering a global recession. Economic contagion is now spreading as fast as the disease itself."[43]

While recognizing the hazards of forecasting as the disease progresses, the authors consider potential scenarios. They hearken back to the global financial crisis of twelve years ago to illustrate how it led to "recessions with vastly different progressions and recoveries in three sample countries: Canada, United States and Greece."[44] Canada experienced a V-shaped shock to its economy: it avoided a deep and prolonged collapse and recovered to its pre-crisis path. The United States experienced a U-shaped shock: a more protracted and costly one with a continuing negative impact on growth. Greece's experience was the worst: an L-shaped shock that left lasting structural damage to its economy.

The obvious question follows: Where does the coronavirus shock fit in?[45] The writers' analysis leads them to conclude that "the risk profile of the COVID-19 crisis is particularly threatening."[46] As of their writing in March 2020, either a V- or U-shaped shock is plausible, but without medical and policy innovation, "the odds are not in favour of the less damaging V-shaped scenario."[47] The countries – including Canada – that eventually emerge from a U-shaped recession (or worse) may be very different from the countries of today.

In Canada's case, a record deficit and national debt, combined with deficits and debts in the provinces, will constrain governments' efforts to address deteriorating economic conditions that existed before the pandemic as well as those resulting from it. Committing more money, or further redistributing what monies there are, cannot be the answer; we must rely instead on innovation, a field in which Canada's track record is not inspiring. That has to change if our country and its citizens are to prosper.

chapter six

Canadian Institutions and Citizenship

Although in March 2021 Prime Minister Justin Trudeau dismissed the parliament he leads as founded upon "colonialism, or discrimination or systemic racism,"[1] there is a more persuasive account of its weaknesses: Donald Savoie's *Democracy in Canada: The Disintegration of Our Institutions* (2019).[2] Savoie's thesis is that Canada "has what is required to make representative democracy work"[3] – competitive political parties, a free press, a professional public service, and an independent judiciary – but that these "building blocks of representative democracy" are not up to the task.[4] He contends that Canadian democracy confronts four major challenges.

> First, the country's national political institutions remain unable to both address the regional factor in shaping policy and to operate under constitutional conventions that underpin Westminster parliamentary government. Second, government bureaucracy has lost its way, and it is no longer able to meet the expectations of politicians and citizens. Third, the average citizen believes that national political institutions cater to those who serve in them, to economic elites, and to interest groups at their expense. Fourth, accountability in government no longer meets present-day requirements given the rise of the new media, the work of lobbyists, and incessant calls for greater transparency.[5]

Beginning with the House of Commons, Savoie notes that its decline "and the role of MPs, particularly over the past forty years, has been well documented."[6] The "golden rules" for newly elected members who hope to advance their careers are: follow party discipline, do not raise contentious issues in public, and don't create problems for the party leader.[7] In theory, MPs have an important responsibility for controlling public spending, but this power is nominal: "the prime minister and minister of finance – with the emphasis on prime ministers and their courtiers – decide who gets what, end of debate."[8] According to one former member and cabinet minister, parliament and specifically the House of Commons "has allowed its most vital power, the power of the purse, to become a dead letter, their supply and estimates process an empty ritual."[9]

We might expect the cabinet – those chosen by the prime minister to head ministries or to serve as associates or without portfolio – to lead in the House of Commons and to make vital decisions, but one former minister contends that "cabinet is not a decision-making body, it is a focus group for the prime minister."[10] Savoie's verdict is blunt: "cabinet government is failing."[11] It does not make policy; it does not make important decisions; and it has failed, in recent years, to represent the country's regions.[12] Today, prime ministers increasingly rely on senior officials in their office and in the Privy Council. "The Cabinet's failings have wide implications for representative democracy, for accountability, and for our constitution."[13]

The Senate's shortcomings have been discussed publicly for years and so are more widely known to Canadians. It has "confronted a crisis of legitimacy for much of its existence."[14] Its role has been variously described as devoting "sober second thought" to House of Commons deliberations; serving as a voice of regional interests; and providing a forum for Canadians whose gender or minority status leaves them underrepresented in democratic processes. Its successes have been modest and overshadowed by its perceived weaknesses, including, at least until recently, a flawed appointments process.[15] Fundamental reform has proved elusive.

Central to these institutions, as David Smith reminds us,[16] is that Canada is a constitutional monarchy. The Crown is more than an ornament of ceremonial importance; it is woven into constitutional law and practice and "is an index both of the history of Canadian development as a federation and as an autonomous member of the Commonwealth."[17] Misunderstandings about the Crown, the House of Commons, and the Senate – which together constitute Canada's Parliament – and about how each relates to the others, "confound debate and complicate efforts to conceive reform."[18] Notwithstanding, Smith observes, few Canadians "would dissent from the proposition that Canada has one of the world's most enduring and successful constitutions. It is among a handful of countries that existed in 1914 and retain the same form of government as then. Peaceful constitutional evolution is the accepted Canadian way, to such a degree that the political system too often is thought to be unchanging and unchangeable."

This, Smith argues, is a false impression.[19] The adoption of the Charter of Rights and Freedoms and of a formula for amending the constitution, and the recognition of existing Aboriginal and treaty rights, "offer contrary evidence to the sense of stasis that critics claim."[20]

Backdropping the views of both Savoie and Smith are indicators that Canadians are losing confidence in their democratic institutions. Former Supreme Court Chief Justice Beverley McLachlin has observed that "we live in a time when public confidence in individuals and institutions is under siege,"[21] and a succession of recent surveys and polls have found a decline in trust and confidence such that in Canada today, a majority of citizens say they don't trust their civic institutions.[22] As Chrystia Freeland (now Canada's deputy prime minister) wrote in 2011, the trend is international: "When it comes to countries, these days the world's gloomy ones have a lot in common. From Fukushima to Athens, and from Washington to Wenzhou, China, the collective refrain is that government doesn't work."[23] And not only government, writes American Yuval Levin, but institutions generally. He believes that Americans are experiencing a social crisis, one that "has followed upon a collapse of our confidence in institutions – public, private, civic and political."[24]

These are ominous appraisals – particularly for Canada, the country of "peace, order and good government," in which institutions have historically enjoyed robust confidence and trust. The "how and "why" questions point to issues identified by Savoie and Smith, and there is more to the story. David Johnston, former Governor General and president of two of the country's leading universities, attributes the current lack of trust to three "interlocking trends."[25] First, it is "a consequence of the collapse of the liberal democratic consensus in the West that stayed largely intact for some five decades following the end of the Second World War."[26] Second, it is a reaction "to the income stagnation and economic inequalities brought on by globalization in trade and commerce."[27] Third, it "is a product of the digital age that has made information limitless, and communication not merely instantaneous but also constant."[28] This age "was meant to connect and enlighten us. And it has. Yet it has also amplified our anger, stoked our fears, and indulged our pessimism; all of this often overrides connectedness and enlightenment, and mischief-makers have encouraged all three trends in order to undermine our trust in our public institutions and one another."[29]

Canada has three levels of government, so we should ask whether provinces and municipalities have experienced declines in confidence similar to those affecting Ottawa. Evidence is incomplete and dated, but the answer may be yes in the case of provinces and no for municipalities. An Ipsos poll in 2012 found that "Canadians have more trust for their local municipal governments than their provincial or federal governments, and also believe they get better value for the taxes they pay from their local government."[30] Of course, given that Canada has ten provinces three territories and thousands of municipalities, variabilities are many and generalizations must be cautious. It is safe to infer, though, that none of our governing institutions are immune from the decline in trust and confidence noted earlier.

In discharging the responsibilities of government, those elected to the House of Commons or provincial legislatures, or appointed to Senate, are joined by the public service. The Government of Canada is the country's largest single employer, and provincial governments are the largest employers in their respective jurisdictions, with hundreds of thousands of employees from coast to coast to coast. Anyone whose work intersects with government understands the importance of the public service, be it in service delivery or in in accessing decision-makers. Public service officials advise governments, and the best of them abide by the dictum of "advising fearlessly and executing faithfully." They know the sectors in which they work and the actors in the sector, and they understand the context in which decisions must be made. Governments and those they serve suffer if they do not do their work well.

Donald Savoie has studied the public service for decades, and his view carries weight that the federal government bureaucracy has lost its way and is unable to meet the expectations of politicians and citizens:

> Senior public servants have been on the defensive for the past forty years or more. Since the early 1980's, public servants have been told repeatedly that with regard to management they do not measure up to their private sector counterparts. Those who hold political power today have a greater say in shaping policy and striking decisions than was held thirty years ago. In short, the verdict from politicians has been that public servants are not up to task on either policy or managing government operations."[31]

They are also seen as occupying privileged and protected positions that are immune from the pressures of a competitive global economy. Reform efforts either have fallen short or have come to naught.

Edelman, an international public relations and marketing firm, has been publishing its trust barometer for twenty years. Its 2020 report was an online survey of more than 34,000 respondents in twenty-eight markets conducted before the pandemic appeared in our lives. The barometer reveals that "despite a strong global economy and near full employment, none of the four societal institutions that the study measures – government, business, NGOs and media – is trusted."[32] In developed markets trust levels are driven primarily by income inequality. "A majority of respondents in every developed market do not believe they will be better off in five years' time, and more than half of respondents globally believe that capitalism in its current form is now doing more harm than good in the world."[33] In the Canadian market, the findings are consistent with the global results: there is a notable trust gap between the informed and uninformed publics, with the latter distrustful of all four institutions measured.[34]

The pandemic may alter trust sentiment for the better in the short term. In May 2020, two observers claimed that the COVID-19 crisis "has ushered in a 'Team Canada' spirit" in which "the unprecedented levels of cooperation taking place between Ottawa and the provinces in tackling the pandemic have been inspiring."[35] The impact in the longer term – for Canada and the globe – is more difficult to anticipate. Dutch historian Rutger Bregman writes that the pandemic has brought on "the biggest societal shake up since the second world war,"[36] and if he is correct, the many issues on the table will include all of the reasons for the decline of trust in our institutions.

Among entities that are important for democratic life are universities, and as of 2017, they were bucking the trend of declining support for societal institutions. In that year, Abacus Data undertook a nationwide survey, commissioned by Universities Canada, to determine how Canadians felt about their universities.[37] A large majority (78%) expressed positive sentiments generally, with substantial majorities favourably disposed to their research and operations. These numbers held between 2015 and 2017; if they have held since, universities represent an important exception to the downward trends reviewed so far in this chapter.

George Fallis has called for universities to be recognized as "integral institutions of liberal democracy."[38] By this he does not mean greater democracy in their internal governance, an abandonment of elite standards, or alignment with progressive causes. He means that universities should "have an explicit mission to contribute to democratic life."[39] That mission has been implicit in many of their activities: accessible university education, liberal undergraduate education, the role of professors as public intellectuals, the responsibility of universities to serve "as critic and conscience in a democratic society"[40] and to generate new knowledge and assess its impact – all of these speak to democratic obligations.

Fallis argues that they must be made explicit and that universities need to be held accountable for how well they meet them.[41] He cites Robert Dahl's concern that the media, political parties, interest groups, and traditional institutions of primary and secondary education do not equip citizens for civic responsibilities in the modern era. Universities "can enhance the older institutions and provide new means for civic education, political participation, information and deliberation."[42] They build on what Amy Gutman described as "a responsibility ... to develop democratic character,"[43] but the "fundamental democratic purpose of a university is protection against the tyranny of ideas. Control of the creation of ideas – whether by a majority or minority – subverts democracy."[44]

This writer is among those who have expressed concerns about some in our universities who undermine rather than advance their democratic role.[45] Weakened Enlightenment values and a rush to judgment through social media; the relegation of freedom of expression to a competing value rather than a first principle; moral absolutism and activism bent on turning the university mission into a social justice crusade – all of these threaten the central role of universities, which is to seek truth. That role they must honour to meet their democratic obligations.

We should be encouraged that Canadian universities retain wide public support, but we must not be blasé about findings of dysfunction in other institutions and the diminishing trust in them. Neither Canada nor liberal democracy in general can be taken for granted. Harvard University's Steven Levitsky and Daniel Ziblatt write that democracies die in different ways.[46] Often they dissolve "in spectacular fashion, through military power and coercion." A coup d'état is the classic example. Sometimes they die "at the hands ... of elected leaders ... who subvert the very process that brought them to power,"[47] and again, there is a classic example: Germany at the hands of Hitler in 1933–34. Sometimes, too, "democracies erode slowly, in barely visible steps."[48]

Levitsky and Ziblatt's concern is with their own country, the United States. They know that its constitution, commitment to freedom and equality, historically strong middle class, prosperity,

high levels of education, and strong private sector[49] should allevi-
ate their concern:

> Yet, we worry. American politicians now treat their rivals as enemies,
> intimidate the free press, and threaten to reject the results of elections.
> They try to weaken the institutional buffers of our democracy
> including the courts, intelligence services, and ethics offices. American
> states, which were once praised by the great jurist Louis Brandeis as
> "laboratories of democracy" are in danger of becoming laboratories
> of authoritarianism as those in power rewrite electoral laws, redraw
> constituencies, and even rescind voting rights to ensure that they do
> not lose.[50]

Canadians should share their worry, for two reasons. First, the
United States is Canada's neighbour and friend, and its influence
does not stop at the border between our two countries. Second,
though few would see Canadian politics in terms similar to those
set out by Levitsky and Ziblatt in the United States, there is a dis-
temper in our public life that could be exploited or that might
evolve in a similar direction.

Conclusion

Institutions matter. They house the governance of our vast, decentralized federal state and our democratic processes. They endeav-
our to balance needs and requests, deliver services, and resolve
differences. They represent Canada in its relations with the rest of
the world, and they are important symbols of our aspirations as a
country and as Canadian citizens. We need effective and respected
institutions, and we are falling short on both counts. The severity of shortcomings and their causes are debatable, but we cannot
sidestep the issues.

The global context is an aggravating factor. Many writers have
described the decline of institutions and of confidence in them
as an international phenomenon driven by economic insecurity,
inequality, and a lack of confidence that concerted efforts are under

way to address them. A leadership vacuum adds to the problem. Why are we not tackling the well-documented failings of parliament and of cabinet government? Why have efforts to reform the public service yielded only modest results? What plans do we have to address gaps and deficits in trust?

The decline of institutions and of confidence in them undermines citizenship, at least in the sense understood by Alan Cairns. A linking mechanism binding citizens to the state and to one another is weakened by diminished institutions and absence of trust. Unless these issues are successfully addressed they will add to pressures on our citizenship.

chapter seven

What Is to Be Done?

The language is becoming more pointed. "Are we a country, or are we not?," queried one national columnist, expressing incredulity about the suspension of parliament in May 2020 until late in the year.[1] The question may come to mind more often as we reflect on the themes and issues considered in this book. We have seen that questions persist about a weak national identity vis-à-vis strong provincial ones. We have witnessed a more pronounced east–west divide in the wake of the 2019 election, one certain to be exacerbated by the demographics of an aging population and unevenness in provincial capacities to address them. We have experienced a growth of identity politics facilitated and fuelled by social media. There is tension in our reconciliation process after rail blockages and protests that led more than two thirds of Canadians to think of their country as broken. The fundamentals of the Canadian economy are mediocre, and the country lacks an internationally competitive industrial strategy.[2] The flaws in our institutions are accompanied by declining confidence in them. The international context is influenced by populism, diminished Enlightenment values, and a shortage of trust throughout much of the developed world – and all this before the pandemic arrived on our shores. Indeed, the question is, what is to be done?

Some may say that the question and its antecedents are unduly provocative. Countries tend to endure and find ways to address problems or to live with them. As David Smith points out, Canada has been among the most durable since the early years of the twentieth century,[3] and there is recent evidence that most Canadians prize their citizenship.[4] What appears to be different now – at least to this writer –is the number and magnitude of issues that act as centrifugal influences upon our citizenship, sending us to our respective corners, wary of meeting in the centre. Andrew Potter writes that "a democracy is nothing more, and nothing less, than a committed relationship between citizens and their political institutions. It is a shared set of expectations, hopes and dreams, with a plan for how they might be accomplished."[5] Are we confident, in 2020, that this committed relationship is in place along with the expectations, hopes, and dreams we share as Canadians?

The work of Elizabeth Anderson, ten years ago, was referenced in the introduction to this book. She observed that Americans had "forgotten the value of identification with a larger nation-wide community," and she urged her fellow citizens "to restore integration to a central place" on their political agenda.[6] She is not alone in these or similar sentiments. Mark Lilla urged fellow liberals in the United States to again speak of citizenship: "What's crucial at this juncture in our history is to concentrate on this shared political status, not on our other manifest differences."[7] Francis Fukuyama foresees integration as "the remedy for the populist politics of the present."[8] The liberal democratic values cherished by Steven Pinker and others are predicated on robust citizenship.

Anderson's central concern is inequality, "the persistence of large, systematic, and seemingly intractable disadvantages that track lines of group identity, along with troubling patterns of intergroup interaction that call into question our claim to be a fully democratic society of equal citizens."[9] She describes as illusory the belief that equality can be achieved "through, or at least notwithstanding, substantial racial segregation."[10] Integration, she argues, "promotes greater equality and democracy. Hence, it is an imperative of justice. It is also a positive good … Integration in a diverse society expands our networks of cooperation and provides a stepping stone to a cosmopolitan identity, which offers the prospect of rewarding relations with people across the globe."[11]

Integration is not assimilation by another name:

> The ideal of integration does not call for the elimination of group difference or group identity, nor for sweeping prohibitions on ethnocentric affiliation, nor for the elimination of institutions in which stigmatized groups constitute a majority. In a just society, the fate of such identities and affiliations can be left to the free choice of equals. Integration does call for full participation of members of salient social groups on terms of equality, cooperation and mutual respect in all domains of civil society ... It requires the construction of a superordinate group identity, a "we" from the perspective of which cooperative goals are framed, and appropriate policies selected and implemented. In a democratic society, this "we" is most importantly a shared identity as citizens."[12]

The "we" is not important to everyone. For some theorists, according to Sharon Stanley, "the battle for racial integration appears to represent the bygone era of the 1950s and 1960s Civil Rights Movement,"[13] with the years since provoking "increasing pessimism about integration, both as a feasible goal and as a worthy ideal."[14] Whether the pessimists ignore citizenship, take it for granted, or accept it as a casualty of turning away from integration, the topic has receded from public view in the United States and in Canada. We noted in chapter 1 that citizenship is rarely invoked in the name of national policy, leading us to wonder whether such an invocation is even possible. "Who speaks for Canada?," queried Trudeau the elder during the 1980 referendum on Quebec secession. What would the answer be if the question were repeated today?

All Canadians have in common their eligibility to carry the same passport. For some of us, as noted earlier, this may be the extent of our attachment to Canada, but most of us see greater value in our country. We have attachments to the reality and/or the idea of Canada that are as variable as those who have them, and that variability shifts and adjusts over time according to changes in the country or in our lives. Once we begin to speak of common citizenship, we become interested in overlapping attachments, or what we share as citizens that gives us an affinity with one another in this vast, diverse, and decentralized land. It is the concept of overlapping attachments that points to the most important question underlying this volume: how do most Canadians feel about their citizenship?

The answer to Trudeau the elder's question is that most Canadians speak for Canada, and it is the responsibility of our leaders to give them – and sometimes help them find – voice. This is not an easy task, because majorities do not consist of fixed members and numbers vary – sometimes sharply – in different regions and provinces and at different times. Occasionally we invoke the language of a "silent majority" to express this idea of overlapping and shared sentiments that are unvoiced or unheard in a wider crowd. That term is somewhat cliché, but it does express a sense that there is majoritarian sentiment in addition to the minority and sometimes sectarian views that are often more prominent in the public commons and that this majoritarian sentiment is essential to the life of the country. When we inquire how most Canadians feel about their citizenship, it is this majoritarian sentiment we seek to uncover.

Here lies a problem. When the prime minister says that the country lacks a core identity or mainstream, or he and others assert that we are defined by our differences, they downplay the importance of overlapping attachments that underlie citizenship. This can be exploited by those set on destructive agendas. Only twenty-five years ago a charismatic Quebec leader – Lucien Bouchard – declared that Canada was not a real country, and he brought it to the edge of dissolution in the second Quebec independence referendum in fifteen years. He was in effect saying, much like René Lévesque declared in the 1980 referendum, that the differences between Quebec and the rest of Canada warranted expression in different countries. That reasoning does not apply only to Quebec; some have observed that parts of western Canada are only a charismatic leader away from making western alienation a threat to our unity. And we have seen in this volume that there are currents of thought on Indigenous issues that could lead in a similar direction. If it is our differences that define us, we may end up in different places.

In 2020–21, the COVID-19 pandemic has thrown us into a new space. All our lives have been disrupted, and our preoccupations have become immediate in the struggle with the contagion's impacts. Governments have clearly responded, spending many billions of dollars on their citizens' most pressing needs, and Canadians feel a sense of solidarity as they face problems of common origin. But whether the pandemic lasts months or years, our differences will eventually resurface, and they will be exacerbated – probably by recession and certainly by constraints born of public spending on the virus. And when they do resurface, the question "What is to be done?" will return to mind.

We consider again the words of Andrew Potter. A democracy "is a shared set of expectations, hopes and dreams, with a plan for how they might be accomplished."[15]

If this definition is compelling enough, we might use it as a guide as we approach to the questions raised in previous chapters: (1) Is our understanding of citizenship changing, and if so, what are the consequences? (2) Must we counter populism and declining Enlightenment values? (3) Is reconciliation with Indigenous peoples on a secure path within our federation? (4) Will present and future newcomers be welcome in Canada? (5) Do fiscal tensions threaten Canadian citizenship? (6) Is reform to our public institutions necessary and a realistic prospect? The rest of this chapter is organized around suggested answers to these questions.

Is our understanding of citizenship changing, and if so, with what consequences? It is changing. We have seen that there are different conceptions of our citizenship that have varying implications for how we see the country. Alan Cairns viewed it as a linking mechanism between citizens, and between them and the state, and he worried that the links were weakening. Multicultural citizenship, he believed, should not give way to multinational citizenship within Canada. Peter Russell argues that this has happened: we do not have a common sense of civic identity; rather, we occupy a common political space with ongoing negotiation of the terms on which it is shared. His argument brings to mind an instrumental approach "in which citizenship loses its nationalist, state-sanctifying aura"[16] and becomes a "tool" that enables pursuit of individual interests.[17] Others subscribe to identity politics and pay little or no attention to citizenship at all, either because it doesn't interest them or because they are focused on those with whom they share identities of race, religion, ideology, gender, sexual orientation, or other particulars.

In this spring of 2021, Cairns's approach is compatible with the idea of shared expectations, hopes, and dreams. Russell's approach may also be, though it is provisional and dependent on the negotiable terms by which Canadians share the space that is Canada. The severe variant of identity politics is incompatible with it, though milder forms are not if they focus on combating discrimination to enable equal participation in the shared expectations, hopes, and dreams of one's fellow citizens. There is another approach, this one voiced by Jennifer Welsh, who in 2004 asserted that Canada "has the potential to be a model citizen for the twenty-first century."[18] Describing the country in this way reflected her view that "although citizenship is something that is given to individuals, it's a fundamentally social concept. It doesn't make sense outside of a collective framework."[19] Her words can be viewed as a precursor to Will Kymlicka and Kathryn Walker's investigation of rooted cosmopolitanism, which links local attachments of national citizenship to a "normative conception of global community, responsibility and governance."[20]

This concept of rooted cosmopolitanism merits a closer look. Notably, Kymlicka and Walker contradict Prime Minister Justin Trudeau's assertion that Canada is the world's first post-national state:[21] "There can be no question of the enduring power of national identities and loyalties within Canada. Compared with other Western democracies, Canadians express above-average levels of national pride and identity. We are not at all a post-national society that has renounced or transcended the identities and practices of nationhood."[22] But the ways in which we accommodate and practise those identities makes us potentially well-suited to rooted cosmopolitanism. First, "the politics of diversity within Canada connects Canadians to those beyond our borders, yet without threatening the integrity of the state."[23] Second, as a middle power, "we are dependent on international rules and alliances for our security and prosperity."[24] And third, although our history records blemishes and failures, we also have "a long history of Canadian commitments to cosmopolitan ideals."[25] Canada is "an interesting test case for ideas of rooted cosmopolitanism."[26] That said, a *successful* case will require the engagement of most Canadians and of both federal and provincial governments. We might add that if universities follow George Fallis's suggestion that contributions to democratic life be added to their missions, the idea of rooted cosmopolitanism merits inclusion in that project.

In our reflections on each of the six questions just outlined, we should consider measures that might enhance our citizenship. Three are offered here for consideration: a requirement that Canadian citizens of voting age present themselves to vote in federal elections; a lowering of the voting age to sixteen; and the creation of a Team Canada of younger Canadians to better familiarize them with our vast country. The first is not a new idea; several countries require their citizens to vote, and the present Canadian government has promised to consider that step, one that as Paul Thomas observes "raises interesting philosophical, legal, political and administrative issues."[27] Those in favour of it argue that it would lead to higher voter turnouts and a more representative voting population; those who are against it argue that it would be an infringement of liberty, that it would bring larger numbers of uninformed voters to the polls, and that it would raise difficult legal and administrative questions. Thomas is not definitive on the issue, seeing "no compelling reason to adopt [compulsory voting] in Canada at this time."[28]

The infringement-of-liberty argument is not compelling. It is reasonable to require of citizens that they present themselves to vote. If they don't like the names on the ballot, they may despoil it, not mark it, or write in another name. (If large numbers chose to do so, that alone would be significant). However, eligible voters would have to present their hidden ballots to returning officers for deposit in the ballot box in order to meet their obligation; what they recorded on the ballot would remain their business alone.

Nor (as Thomas points out) is the argument about uninformed voters compelling. Some who vote now may be unfamiliar with the issues, and in any event, the uninformed – whether previous or new voters – may become informed. Compulsory voting would require adjustments on the part of political parties and the media to broaden their reach to better include all potential voters. It would also require a change of mindset on the part of voters, many of whom would have to direct their attention to the choices before them.

The Australian experience may be the most germane to Canada. It is a large federation with institutions similar to ours. More than 90 per cent of eligible Australian voters typically cast their ballots, a much higher percentage than the 67 per cent of Canadians who voted in 2019 and the 55 per cent of Americans who did so in the 2016 presidential election. Elections in Australia are always held on Saturdays, often in conjunction with picnics or other community events. In the words of one participant, "voting in Australia is like a party. There's a BBQ at the local school. Everyone turns up. Everyone votes. There's a sense that: We're all in this together. We're all affected by the decisions we make today."[29] The country has nearly a century of experience with compulsory voting, and the practice is unlikely to change.

Our contemplation of compulsory voting should also lead us to ask whether an earlier voting age might also be appropriate. Those in favour of a right to vote beginning at sixteen point to the potential of earlier engagement with political issues and to a stronger commitment to voting thereafter; those opposed argue that sixteen-year-olds lack the experience and maturity to join the voting public. Evidence is not definitive either way, though we note that modest experience to date, particularly in the European Community, has been positive, with little pushback to reverse the trend. Such a change would have to be accompanied by better civic preparation in high school on the history of democracy and on voting processes, but the case for earlier voting should be allowed at least a trial period.

A third measure that might enhance our citizenship would be to create a Team Canada to enable young Canadians to learn about and serve their country. The power of knowing the country better should not be underestimated. Size, diversity, and natural endowment are defining features of Canada; those who have experienced them have an indelible sense of what they mean to the country, other Canadians, and the places where they live. There has been some interprovincial migration – particularly east to west – for employment reasons, and there are some exchange programs, but the experience of most Canadians is local or regional. Even a great majority of undergraduate post-secondary students attend institutions in their home cities or provinces. The colloquial invitation to "get out more" should extend to young people to get out of their home towns, provinces, and regions to experience more of the vast country in which we live.

The underlying idea of this is not new. The short-lived Company of Young Canadians was established in 1966 in anticipation of Canada's centennial but fell victim to poor organization only nine years later. The more successful World University Service of Canada (WUSC) has an international focus aimed at disadvantaged youth, and the Canadian University Service Overseas (CUSO) focuses on emerging nations. The difference here is that the Team Canada proposal would engage young Canadians interested in knowing their *own* country better.

Different models could serve the purpose. An NGO developed along the lines of the successful WUSC is one. Another could be for post-secondary students to apply to Citizenship and Immigration Canada for internships in a region other than the one they grew up in or where they currently live. The federal government would administer the program, working with provinces, businesses, and NGOs to develop an inventory of internship opportunities. Those selected would receive a stipend to cover their travel and living expenses. Whatever the model, program design would be key to achieving its purpose.

Must we counter populism and declining Enlightenment values? This second question draws us into some of the most contested issues of the modern era. Us-versus-them politics are on the rise, and this trend is likely to accelerate as Western liberal democratic thought continues to be assailed by ideological and cultural foes who are placing Enlightenment themes and values – reason, science, humanism, and progress – at risk. Populism is but one manifestation of this assault, pitting citizens against one another with divisive, belligerent rhetoric and threatening postures, but Canadians have thus far escaped the worst of its influence. But populism is not the only threat to Enlightenment values; more broadly, as we learn from Stephen Bronner, they are under assault from across the political spectrum,[30] and Queen's University's Bruce Pardy argues that Canadian law and society are among those threatened.[31]

Underpinning this assault is a fallacy, albeit a powerful one: ways of *thinking* and *learning* are routinely described as ways of *knowing*. If this were a mere figure of speech it would be harmless, but it is more. Western rationality – with its insistence on evidence, reason, and conclusions founded on both – is seen by some as simply one "way of knowing," as if there were other ways specific to different cultural, racial, religious, gender, and other social identities. Seen in an epistemological context, this is understandable: different voices and different ways of thinking and learning enrich our understanding. However, elevating ways of thinking and learning to "ways of knowing" is exclusionary; it sets them up in competition with one another. You have your way of knowing, I have mine. You have your truth, I have mine.

This is anti-intellectual and divisive. It is evident even in our universities, and any doubt on this matter could be tested by a poll that asked faculty, staff, and students whether they have witnessed a growing intolerance of pluralism and liberal democratic rationality in the halls of academia. We might be troubled by the high numbers who would say yes.

Is reconciliation with Indigenous peoples on a secure path within our federation? As we saw in chapter 3, the answer to this third question is mixed. Canadians have a better understanding of their history; most are supportive of reconciliation, and important steps have been taken in this direction. But progress remains modest, rail blockades have been setbacks, and governance issues are in the way. Of concern, too, is that some contemporary Indigenous scholars have little interest in either Canada or its state-sponsored programs to better Indigenous lives. Either they have never looked for constructive engagement with Canada or they have given up on it.

But there are reasons for optimism, which are supported by a recent Environics survey of young Indigenous and non-Indigenous Canadians between the ages of sixteen and twenty-nine.[32] Each group reported growing numbers of interactions with the other that "are comfortable most or all of the time," as well as growing numbers of friendships between them. Furthermore, "three-quarters (75%) of non-Indigenous youth believe that Indigenous peoples are often or sometimes subject to discrimination in Canadian society; the proportion of Indigenous youth who perceive discrimination is higher, but not dramatically so, at 84%."[33] The Environics report goes on: "What about how to move forward? Indigenous and non-Indigenous youth define reconciliation in similar terms. In both groups, the most common definitions of reconciliation are 'rebuilding relationships/trust,' 'apology/making amends,' and 'repairing/correcting past wrongs.' In both groups, significant majorities are optimistic about seeing meaningful reconciliation in their lifetimes: 73 percent of Indigenous youth and 68 percent of non-Indigenous youth."[34]

If young people are our best hope, then this survey gives us more reasons for optimism. The numbers are encouraging, and so is the belief among those surveyed that the Truth and Reconciliation Commission offers a path forward – rebuilding relationships and acknowledging and repairing past wrongs. Their hopes do not rest on unlikely prospects of major constitutional change or a reordering of Canadian federalism. The survey suggests that these young people envision a future of Indigenous and non-Indigenous peoples together, based on equality and achievable measures to bring it about.

To the question "What is to be done?," this is the most important part of the answer: reconciliation must continue until we can say that Indigenous and non-Indigenous Canadians are participating as equal citizens in the unfolding story of Canada. While important progress has been made, most of the reconciliation process is ahead of us.

Another part of the answer relates to governance (see chapter 3). Recall that with the Coastal GasLink Pipeline protests, Theresa Tait-Day – a Wet'suwet'en hereditary chief shorn of her title because of her support for the pipeline – raised governance issues later cast by former Justice Minister Jody Wilson-Raybould in the form of this question: "Who represents Indigenous peoples in Canada?"[35] As seen earlier, John Graham, a governance consultant who has worked with Indigenous communities for twenty-five years, outlined the issues as he had experienced them.

In general, Governance has been topical for the past two decades. The 2001 bankruptcy of Enron and the dissolution of audit and accountancy giant Arthur Anderson touched off widespread reviews and reforms of governance in organizations throughout the Western world. In 2002 the Government of Canada introduced the First Nations Governance Act in the House of Commons, legislation that would have amended the Indian Act "to require bands to design and adopt codes for leadership selection, the administration of government, and financial management and accountability."[36] The legislation was not well-received by Indigenous leaders and was subsequently abandoned. In 2013 the Harper government enacted the 2013 First Nations Financial Transparency Act, but its effect was short-lived; shortly after taking office the Trudeau government announced that it would not enforce the legislation.

The goal of Indigenous self-determination has not been controversial in today's Canada. But there have long been divergent views as to what it means and what its reach should be. For some it means sovereignty with independence; for most it means greater control for Indigenous peoples over their daily lives, services, and lands. Independence is theoretically possible though unimaginable in practice: we are all Canadian citizens with complex interrelationships and with Charter rights and freedoms that belie the idea of going our separate ways. Greater Indigenous control over lives, services, and lands is achievable though its extent will vary depending on the particulars of different First Nations. It is subject to negotiations between those nations and the Canadian government, and the need for such talks is ever more urgent. Governance issues – transparency, accountability, and responsibility – must be part of these negotiations. Their resolution will provide a more secure foundation for reconciliation.

Will present and future newcomers be welcome in Canada? Indigenous peoples initially welcomed newcomers to what is now Canada, but over time they were overwhelmed by their numbers and abused by them. After the initial French and English colonizers, newcomers of many different cultures and nationalities came to the country, resulting in the multicultural mosaic we have today. How will future newcomers be received?

It is clear from the discussion in chapter 4 that Canadian policy will not be embracing either extreme of the spectrum between completely closed and completely open borders. Immigration will depend on an ongoing conversation among Canadians and between them and their leaders, and because the subject can be exploited for narrow or xenophobic reasons, the conversation should rise above partisanship. Confidence in the numbers and processes by which newcomers are admitted to the country is essential for sound immigration policy.

It is also clear that substantial immigration will be needed for economic reasons and to meet the country's demographic challenges. The actual numbers are debatable, but recent experience suggests that they are appropriate at this time – around one third of a million per year. Of course, our policies will not be of interest only to ourselves; the international community will be watching them too. Our size, population density, and wealth make us visible in the world of global immigration, and we must be seen to be doing our share in addressing the population movements that can be expected in years to come.

Migration generated by population growth and climate change is unpredictable, but the numbers could be high. Contrasting views on the planet's population point either to an increase to about nine billion by mid-century, followed by decline (Ibbitson and Bricker), or to increasing numbers throughout the century and possibly beyond. Either will challenge earth's resources, but the latter forecast (by the UN Department of Economic and Social Affairs) would see more than 3.5 billion people added to our numbers in the next eighty years. When we consider that climate change may soon make some heavily populated areas of the globe uninhabitable, we can envision migrations in the millions as people move to find habitable space. Large First World countries, including Canada, will be popular destinations, and the ongoing conversation of Canadians on newcomers should anticipate this possibility.

Do fiscal tensions threaten Canadian citizenship? Our fifth question directs us to Richard Saillant's expectation of a poorer, older east and a wealthier, younger west. A combination of government debt and recession in the post-pandemic world will hinder our capacity to address the disparity, and the equalization formula will be challenged by donor provinces, whose altered circumstances will make it difficult to sustain. The Alberta government has already promised a referendum in 2021 on removing equalization from the constitution to seek leverage in negotiating a new deal with Ottawa.

No single province can end equalization; it is a federal program enshrined in our constitution and widely supported in principle. But Alberta's grievances should not be dismissed as mere pique or incipient separatism. Albertans have been the greatest per capita contributors to equalization courtesy of an energy industry that has little support in the federal government and that is vilified by many who have been its beneficiaries. Alberta also contributes more than its share per capita to other programs, including Employment Insurance and the Canada Pension Plan. The difference now is that Albertans' fiscal capacity to be lead per capita contributors to these programs has been compromised by body blows to its primary industry, and by the pandemic, and their calls for reform will only intensify.

In 2018 the federal government quietly extended the current equalization formula to 2024 despite calls for change in Ontario and the west. Those calls should now be heeded, not delayed until 2024. The program's delivery mechanisms should also be addressed. The federal government should relinquish the program's administration to an arm's length agency, comprised of experts in Canadian fiscal federalism, that will determine payments and adjust the formula. This agency should review equalization in other federal states and make recommendations to the governments of Canada and all the provinces on best practices, which should be reflected in equalization and other redistributive programs.

Interprovincial trade is another source of economic tensions within Canada. In an era that has featured the relentless pursuit of international free trade agreements by Canadian leaders, we continue to tolerate domestic trade barriers that make it easier for foreign interests to do business across Canada than domestic ones. The Canadian Free Trade Agreement of 2017 may bring change, though at present it is delivering less than its title promises. It is a framework agreement, but one that should be put on a fast track to deliver trade within Canada that is freed from both tariff and most current non-tariff barriers.

The fundamentals of the Canadian economy may constrain us further in our response to current pressures. Our competitiveness, productivity, innovation, levels of debt, and business investment were unimpressive going into the pandemic and they have not received the public attention and debate they require. They will be even weaker when we leave the virus behind, and the consequences will be felt by all Canadians. They must be addressed for Canada to be competitive with its peer G7 and OECD countries.

Economist Don Drummond has written about Canada's weak economic growth:

> The main reasons for such low growth are the aging population, slowing labour force growth and a continuation of modest productivity gains. Canada looks especially bad from the international perspective as our level of output per capita in 2019 was 3.4 per-cent below The Organization for Economic Co-operation and Development average, 11.4-per-cent below the eurozone and 26.6 per-cent below the United States. We can and must do better.[37]

Drummond proposes the creation of "an institute focusing on strengthening economic growth in an environmentally sustainable manner with the benefits more evenly distributed among the population."[38] It could be a federal government agency but one with "sufficient independence to challenge the status quo."[39] It should be led "by someone with credibility in economic and policy matters"[40] and have research staff and connected research networks as well as an advisory body connected to provincial and municipal governments and other stakeholders.

Drummond's most important message is that the Canadian economy needs concerted and systematic attention from governments. Political parties lack the capacity and perhaps the conviction to generate this attention; their leaders rarely reference business investment, productivity, and growth. Meanwhile, citizens are too often seen as having little competence or interest in them. As the preoccupation with the pandemic recedes, the economy must be top of mind for Canadians and their governments.

Is reform to our public institutions necessary and a realistic prospect? Our final question invites us to consider the prospects for institutional reform. We should expect universities to come to the defence of Enlightenment values and liberal democratic thought. Here, let us return to the work of George Fallis, whose recommendations are more urgent today than when he made them in 2011. Two of his ideas are germane to this discussion: universities should offer a liberal education minor to their undergraduate students; and we should recognize a new social contract between universities and society, one that supports deliberative democracy as well as representative democracy.[41] To these we should add that universities should reflect, and be seen to reflect, in their internal cultures and in their outreach, that freedom of expression supported by scholarly discipline has pride of place among their values.[42]

We have seen, too, that there is wide acknowledgment of the need for change within our institutions of government. The decline in the roles of the House of Commons and the cabinet, and continuing questions about the legitimacy of Senate, are problems at any time, but the pressures on the country now and for the foreseeable future make them acute in 2020. Quebec's support for the country remains muted, and western voices of discontent are now being expressed in a separatist political party – Wexit (now the Maverick Party) – led by a former House of Commons leader in the federal government, Jay Hill. Some voices in Indigenous law and politics have little regard for Canada and Canadian citizenship. Canada's economic performance is mediocre by competitive standards, and its weaknesses will be magnified by the pandemic. Belief in the power of reason and science is waning. We need effective and efficient institutions of government to cope with our many challenges: a House of Commons in which members participate in government rather than follow orders; a cabinet in which members reflect the different regions of Canada and join the prime minister in making decisions rather than serving as a focus group; a Senate more capable of adding voice to the different parts of the country.

If we look back upon Canada's major national achievements in the writer's lifetime, we see how important it was to have determined leadership: the St Lawrence Seaway (St Laurent); the adoption of a new Canadian flag that would become an enduring national symbol (Pearson); the repatriation of the constitution and the Charter of Rights and Freedoms (Trudeau senior); free trade with our most important trading partner (Mulroney). This is the calibre of national leadership that we will need on the road ahead. Whether or not we get it will determine the future of our citizenship, and of our country.

Afterword

On Canada Day 2020, a Halifax daily – the *Chronicle Herald* – apologized for the Canadian flag while newly sworn-in Canadian citizens from around the world explained what drew them to Canada.[1] "I started feeling like I belonged to this country," said one new Canadian. Another reported amazement at the country's inclusiveness. A third was living his "dream of belonging to the Canadian family." Still another announced his delight to be a Canadian citizen. So the enthusiasms ran, and continued: "living in a country that has chosen the hard path of democracy"; hardship that "was worth it to build a life in Canada"; being "struck by the open and welcoming nature of Canadians"; "a chance to give back to Canada and to become a Canadian at the same time." Perhaps, on the eve of Canada Day, the apologists at the *Chronicle Herald* should have hearkened to the voices of our newest Canadians, particularly in view of the tests to which our citizenship will soon be put.

The pandemic has exacted a high toll on the world: more than two hundred million cases and nearly five million deaths. The virus is still on the rise in parts of the world and a fourth wave has followed the first three. No one has been left untouched by its spread, and millions have felt its direct economic impact. It remains a preoccupation for all. "What comes after the pandemic?" is the top-of-mind question for those who look ahead. After conceding the unknowns, we can discern the knowns: high unemployment, massive public debt, edgier regional tensions, industrial and business dislocation, and changes in our occupational and personal lives that may endure after COVID-19 has receded. To date, these impacts have been overshadowed by the imperative of containing the virus. When it begins to abate, our differences will again come into focus, in some cases more sharply than before. There will not be a reversion to a pre-pandemic status quo.

The issues discussed in this volume will challenge every Canadian and all governments as we face some of the hardest choices and difficult adjustments in our modern history. Canada's survival is not guaranteed, though in its favour is the fact that most Canadians – including our newest ones – care about the country and prize its citizenship. Hopefully it will be these Canadians who inspire the answers for our Canada in question.

Notes

Preface

1 Thucydides, *The Peloponnesian War* (Middlesex: Penguin Books, 1954), 147.
2 Alan Cairns, John C. Courtney, Peter MacKinnon, Hans J. Michelmann, and David E. Smith, eds., *Citizenship, Diversity, and Pluralism* (Montreal and Kingston: McGill–Queen's University Press, 1999).
3 Cairns et al., *Citizenship*, 4.
4 Cairns et al., *Citizenship*, cover page.
5 Matt Parke, "Thomas Friedman: Technology is accelerating faster than we can adapt. We can catch up." workingnation.com, 2 August 2017.

Introduction

1 Elizabeth Anderson, *The Imperative of Integration* (Princeton: Princeton University Press, 2010).
2 Anderson, *The Imperative of Integration*, 1.
3 Anderson, *The Imperative of Integration*, 2.
4 Anderson, *The Imperative of Integration*, 3.
5 Mark Kingwell, "Is Canada a nation or a notion?," *Globe and Mail*, 28 April 2018, www.theglobeandmail.com/opinion/article.
6 Trudeau was reported to have made the observation in an October 2016 interview with the *New York Times*. *The Guardian International*, www.theguardian.com/world/2017/Jan/04.
7 See, for example, Edna Paris, "Canada's multiculturalism is our identity," *Globe and Mail*, 27 April 2018, www.theglobeandmail.com/opinion/article.

8 Alan Cairns, *Citizens Plus: Aboriginal Peoples and the Canadian State* (Vancouver: UBC Press, 2001).
9 Richard Saillant, *A Tale of Two Countries: How the Great Demographic Imbalance Is Pulling Canada Apart* (Halifax: Nimbus, 2016).

1. Revisiting Vertical and Horizontal Dimensions of Citizenship

1 John Ibbitson, "Historian Ramsay Cook helped define modern Canada," *Globe and Mail*, 21 July 2016, www.the globeandmail.com.
2 Donald Savoie, "Eastern and Western Canadians are angry – and Ottawa needs to wake-up," *Globe and Mail*, 28 December 2018, www .theglobeandmail.com.
3 Linda Bosniak is a leading American scholar on citizenship. See, in particular, *The Citizen and the Alien: Dilemmas of Contemporary Membership* (Princeton: Princeton University Press, 2008); and "Status Non Citizens" in *The Oxford Handbook on Citizenship*, edited by Ayelet Shachar, Rainer Baubock, Irene Bloemraad, and Maarten Vink, (Oxford: Oxford University Press, 2017). See also Leti Volpp, "Obnoxious to Their Very Nature": Asian Americans and Constitutional Citizenship," 8 Asian Am. L.J. 71 at 71.
4 Peter J. Spiro, "A New International Law of Citizenship," *American Journal of International Law* 105, no. 4 (2011): 694–746.
5 SC 1985, c C-29.
6 All provinces except Quebec.
7 In a 2014 online survey conducted by Leger Marketing for the Assocation of Canadian Studies, the Charter was ranked first of eleven options in response to the question "What keeps Canada united?" www.cp.24.com.
8 Irwin Cotler, "On the Charter's 32nd birthday, let's celebrate our 'revolution in law,'" *Globe and Mail*, 17 April 2014, www.theglobeand mail.com.
9 Volpp, "Obnoxious," 78n3.
10 Canadians of the writer's generation will recall Prime Minister Diefenbaker's declamations on 'One Canada' and Prime Minister Pierre Trudeau rhetorically asking "Who speaks for Canada?" when the country's unity was threatened.
11 Social licence is not a doctrine of Canadian constitutional law though it has been invoked by interest groups and sometimes politicians (Quebec's premier Legault, for example) as if it were. The Macdonald-Laurier Institute's Brian Lee Crowley and Dwight Newman point out the problem: social licence "confers upon a minority the ability to undermine

democracy and the rule of law." https://www.macdonaldlaurier.ca/social-licence-and-canadian-democracy/.

12 Volpp, "Obnoxious," 72.

13 "Canada 150" (2017), www.ipsos.com.

14 Jean-Marc Leger, Jacques Nantel, and Pierre Duhamel, *Cracking the Quebec Code: The 7 Keys to Understanding Quebecers* (Irvine: Juniper, 2016).

15 John Ibbitson, "Can one of the nicest places in the world – Canada – survive what's to come?," *Globe and Mail*, 30 June 2018, www.theglobeandmail.com.

16 www.ipsos.com.

17 First published in 1972, Margaret Atwood's *Survival: A Thematic Guide to Canadian Literature* is a Canadian classic.

18 "Majority across 25 countries say their country is on the wrong track" (2016), www.ipsos.com/Ipsos-mori.

19 Dr Richard Johnston is quoted in "Is the 2019 election Canada's 'nastiest' ever? Not by a long shot," CBC, 17 October 2019, ca.news.yahoo.com.

20 Jacob Dube, "Most Canadians think royals aren't relevant anymore," *National Post*, 18 January 2020.

21 Dube, "Most Canadians."

22 Alan Cairns, John C. Courtney, Peter MacKinnon, Hans J. Michelmann, and David E. Smith, eds., *Citizenship, Diversity, and Pluralism* (Montreal and Kingston: McGill–Queen's University Press, 1999), 4n2.

23 Cairns et al., *Citizenship*, 19.

24 Adam Rubenstein, "Stephen Pinker: Identity Politics Is 'an Enemy of Reason and Enlightenment Values,'" *Washington Examiner*, 15 February 2018, wwww.washingtonexaminer.com. See also Stephen Pinker, *Enlightenment Now: The Case for Reason, Science, Humanism and Progress* (New York: Viking, 2018).

25 Pinker, *Enlightenment Now*.

26 Mark Lilla, *The Once and Future Liberal* (New York: HarperCollins, 2017).

27 Lilla, *The Once and Future Liberal*, 9.

28 Lilla, *The Once and Future Liberal*, 10.

29 Lilla, *The Once and Future Liberal*, 10.

30 Correspondence with the author, 2019.

31 Correspondence with the author, 2019.

32 Roger Cohen, "Boris Johnson and the Coming Trump Victory in 2020," *New York Times*, 13 December 2019, www.nytimes.com.

33 Francis Fukuyama, *Identity: The Demand for Dignity and the Politics of Resentment* (New York: Farrar, Straus and Giroux, 2018).

34 Fukuyama, *Identity*, 170.

35 Fukuyama, *Identity*, 165.
36 Fukuyama, *Identity*, 180.
37 Kwame Anthony Appiah, *The Lies That Bind: Rethinking Identity* (New York: Liveright, 2018).
38 Appiah, *The Lies That Bind*, 218.
39 Appiah, *The Lies That Bind*, 219.
40 Appiah, *The Lies That Bind*, 219.
41 Charles Taylor, *Multiculturalism* (Princeton: Princeton University Press, 1994).
42 Gerald Kernerman and Philip Resnick, eds., *Insiders and Outsiders: Alan Cairns and the Reshaping of Canadian Citizenship* (Vancouver: UBC Press, 2005).
43 Cairns et al., *Citizenship, Diversity and Pluralism*, 10n2.
44 Cairns et al., *Citizenship, Diversity and Pluralism*, 10.
45 Cairns et al., *Citizenship, Diversity and Pluralism*, 11.
46 Cairns et al., *Citizenship, Diversity and Pluralism*, 11.
47 Cairns et al., *Citizenship, Diversity and Pluralism*, 11.
48 Cairns et al., *Citizenship, Diversity and Pluralism*, 6.
49 Peter Russell, "Citizenship in a Multinational Democracy," in Kernerman and Resnick, *Insiders and Outsiders*, 283n38.
50 Russell, "Citizenship."
51 Alexandra Dobrowolsky and Richard F. Devlin, "Of Cairns and Cages? Identity, Democracy, and Alan Cairns," in Kernerman and Resnick, *Insiders and Outsiders*, 297.
52 Dobrowolsky and Devlin, "Of Cairns and Cages?," 298.
53 Dobrowolsky and Devlin, "Of Cairns and Cages?," 303.
54 Dobrowolsky and Devlin, "Of Cairns and Cages?," 309.
55 Dobrowolsky and Devlin, "Of Cairns and Cages?," 309.
56 Avigail Eisenberg and Will Kymlicka, eds., *Identity Politics in the Public Realm: Bringing Institutions Back In* (Vancouver: UBC Press, 2011).
57 Eisenberg and Kymlicka, *Identity Politics*, 1, 2.
58 Eisenberg and Kymlicka, *Identity Politics*, 9.
59 Eisenberg and Kymlicka, *Identity Politics*, 9.
60 Eisenberg and Kymlicka, *Identity Politics*, 22.
61 Eisenberg and Kymlicka, *Identity Politics*, 22.
62 Eisenberg and Kymlicka, *Identity Politics*, 25.
63 Eisenberg and Kymlicka, *Identity Politics*, 27.
64 Will Kymlicka and Kathryn Walker, eds., *Rooted Cosmopolitanism: Canada and the World* (Vancouver: UBC Press, 2012), 1.
65 Kymlicka and Walker, *Rooted Cosmopolitanism*, 2.
66 Kymlicka and Walker, *Rooted Cosmopolitanism*, 23.
67 Kymlicka and Walker, *Rooted Cosmopolitanism*, 22.

68 Kymlicka and Walker, *Rooted Cosmopolitanism*, 22.
69 For example, the Great Depression and the Second World War.
70 Kymlicka and Walker, *Rooted Cosmopolitanism*, 22.
71 Kymlicka and Walker, *Rooted Cosmopolitanism*, 303n51.
72 Kymlicka and Walker, *Rooted Cosmopolitanism*, 303n56.
73 Christopher Jones-Cruise, "Amnesty International Concerned about 'Us versus Them,'" www.51voa.com.
74 Payam Akhavan, 2017 CBC Massey Lectures, www.cbc.ca.

2. Populism, Enlightenment Values, and Citizenship

1 Amnesty International Secretary General Salil Shetty speaking to reporters upon release of the organization's 2016 report, 23 February 2017, learningenglish.voanews.com.
2 Roger Cohen, "It's Time to Depopularize 'Populist,'" *New York Times*, 13 July 2018, www.nytimes.com.
3 Cas Mudde and Crostobal Rovira Laltwasser, "Voices of the Peoples: Populism in Europe and Latin America Compared," Kellogg Institute Working Paper no. 378, 2011.
4 Mudde and Rovira Laltwasser, "Voices of the Peoples," 9, where the authors credit Freeden (1996) and Laclau (1977).
5 Lane Crothers, "Populism," Brill masthead, brill.com.
6 Norm Gidron and Bart Bonikowski, "Varieties of Populism: Literature Review and Research Agenda" (2013), Working Paper Series, Weatherhead Center for International Affairs, Harvard University, no. 13–0004, 6, https://ssrn.com/abstract=2459387.
7 Gidron and Bonikowski, "Varieties of Populism," 7.
8 Gidron and Bonikowski, "Varieties of Populism," 10.
9 Gidron and Bonikowski, "Varieties of Populism," 14.
10 Gidron and Bonikowski, "Varieties of Populism," 31.
11 Andre Munro, "Populism: Political Program or Movement," *Encyclopedia Britannica*, https://www.britannica.com.
12 Elena Block and Ralph Negrine, "The Populist Communication Style: Toward a Critical Framework," *International Journal of Communication* 11 (2017): 178–97, https://core.ac.uk. See also page 9, where the authors credit Freeden (1996) and Laclau (1977).
13 Block and Negrine, "The Populist Communication Style," 181.
14 Block and Negrine, "The Populist Communication Style," 182.
15 Block and Negrine, "The Populist Communication Style," 182.
16 Michael Hatherall, "Populist Narratives and the Making of National Strategy," *The Bridge* (2018).

17 Hatherall, "Populist Narratives."
18 Simon Bornschier, "Populist Mobilization across Time and Space: An Introduction," *Swiss Political Science Review* 23, no. 4 (2017): 301–12, onlinelibrary.wiley.com.
19 Bornschier, "Populist Mobilization," 305.
20 Bornschier, "Populist Mobilization," 306.
21 Bornschier, "Populist Mobilization," 306.
22 Bornschier, "Populist Mobilization," 306.
23 Claes H. de Vreese, Frank Esser, Toril Aalberg, Carsten Reinemann, and James Stanyer, "Populism as an Expression of Political Communication Content and Style: A New Perspective," *International Journal of Press/ Politics* 23, no. 4 (2018): 423–38 at 424.
24 Cas Mudde, "Populism in the Twenty-First Century: An Illiberal Democratic Response to Undemocratic Liberalism," Penn Arts and Sciences, University of Pennsylvania, 2020, www.sas.upenn.edu.
25 De Vreese et al., "Populism as an Expression," 424n23.
26 De Vreese et al., "Populism as an Expression," 424n23.
27 Clive Cook, "Populists Aren't the Only Enemies of Liberal Democracy," *Bloomberg Opinion*, 1 August 2018, www.bloomberg.com.
28 Moises Naim, "How to Be a Populist," *The Atlantic*, 21 April 2017, www .theatlantic.com.
29 "Populists in Power around the World," Tony Blair Institute for Global Change (2018), www.institute.global/policy.
30 "Populists in Power around the World."
31 Mario Polese, "Why the Populist Surge Has Missed Canada," *City Journal* (2017), www.city-journal.org.
32 David Laycock writes that populism "has a long history in Canada and continues to be an important factor in Canadian political culture and public life. In Canada there have been right wing political parties (e.g. Social Credit Party, Creditistes, Reform) and left-wing populist parties (e.g. United Farmers of Alberta, Co-operative Commonwealth Federation)." David Laycock, "Populism in Canada," *The Canadian Encyclopedia*, 2006, www.thecanadianencyclopedia.ca.
33 Frank Graves and Michael Valpy, "Canada is a tinderbox for populism: The 2019 Election could spark it," *Maclean's*, 3 December 2018, www .macleans.ca.
34 Steven Pinker, *Enlightenment Now: The Case for Reason, Science, Humanism and Progress* (New York: Viking, 2018), 8.
35 Pinker, *Enlightenment Now*, 8, 9.
36 Pinker, *Enlightenment Now*, 5.

37 Pinker, *Enlightenment Now*, 6.
38 Pinker, *Enlightenment Now*, 365.
39 Pinker, *Enlightenment Now*, 5.
40 Pinker, *Enlightenment Now*, book jacket.
41 Albert Saloman, "In Praise of the Enlightenment: In Commemoration of Fontenelle, 1657–1757," *Social Research* 24, no. 2 (Summer 1957), www.jstor.org.
42 Anthony Pagden, *The Enlightenment and Why It Still Matters* (New York: Penguin Random House, 2013) (Kirkus Reviews), www.penguinrandomhouse.com.
43 A.C. Grayling, "How to Defend the Enlightenment: A Full Transcript of the Discussion between Anthony Grayling and Tzvetan Todorov," *New Humanist*, 15 January 2010, newhumanist.org.uk.
44 Dominic Erdozain, "Faith against Faith: Recovering the Religious Character of the Enlightenment" (ABC Religion and Ethics, 2019), www.abc.net.au.
45 Erdozain, "Faith against Faith."
46 Charles Taylor, *A Secular Age* (Cambridge. MA: Harvard University Press, 2007).
47 Phil Badger, "What's Wrong with the Enlightenment," *Philosophy Now*, 2010, philosophynow.org.
48 Stephen Eric Bonner, "Interpreting the Enlightenment: Metaphysics, Critique, and Politics," *Logos Journal*, 2004, logos journal.com.
49 Bonner, "Interpreting the Enlightenment."
50 Bonner, "Interpreting the Enlightenment."
51 Bornschier, "Populist Mobilization," 305.
52 Block and Negrine, "The Populist Communication Style," 181n13.

3. Indigenous Peoples and Citizenship

1 Today estimated to be 4–5 per cent, though a smaller percentage then.
2 J.R. Miller, *Skyscrapers Hide the Heavens: A History of Native–Newcomer Relations in Canada*, 4th ed. (Toronto: University of Toronto Press, 2018).
3 Miller, *Skyscrapers Hide the Heavens*, 41.
4 Miller, *Skyscrapers Hide the Heavens*, 41.
5 Miller, *Skyscrapers Hide the Heavens*, 41.
6 Miller, *Skyscrapers Hide the Heavens*, 345.
7 Miller, *Skyscrapers Hide the Heavens*, 345.
8 Miller, *Skyscrapers Hide the Heavens*, 42.
9 Miller, *Skyscrapers Hide the Heavens*, 347.

10 Miller, *Skyscrapers Hide the Heavens*, 347.
11 Miller, *Skyscrapers Hide the Heavens*, 348.
12 Miller, *Skyscrapers Hide the Heavens*, 348.
13 Miller, *Skyscrapers Hide the Heavens*, 350.
14 Miller, *Skyscrapers Hide the Heavens*, 350.
15 Miller, *Skyscrapers Hide the Heavens*, 350, 351.
16 Miller, *Skyscrapers Hide the Heavens*, 351.
17 J.R. Miller, *Residential Schools and Reconciliation: Canada Confronts Its History* (Toronto: University of Toronto Press, 2017).
18 Miller, *Residential Schools*. Book jacket.
19 John Ivison, "Canada is turning into a mob city while Trudeau remains silent," *National Post*, 12 February 2020.
20 Matthew McClearn, "Back on track: How have Canada's railways and ports been affected?," *Globe and Mail*, 4 March 2020, A11.
21 McClearn, "Back on track," 11.
22 Reported in Chris Selley, "Nothing to sneer at," *Calgary Herald*, 4 March 2020, NP4.
23 *National Post Viewpoint*, 17 February 2020.
24 Thomas J. Courchene, *Indigenous Nationals Canadian Citizens: From First Contact to Canada 150 and Beyond*, Institute of Governmental Relations, School of Policy Studies, Queen's University, Kingston, Ontario, 2018.
25 Courchene, *Indigenous Nationals Canadian Citizens*, 237.
26 Courchene, *Indigenous Nationals Canadian Citizens*, 237.
27 Courchene, *Indigenous Nationals Canadian Citizens*, 237.
28 Courchene, *Indigenous Nationals Canadian Citizens*, 243.
29 Alan Cairns, *Citizens Plus: Aboriginal Peoples and the Canadian State* (Vancouver: UBC Press, 2000).
30 H.B. Hawthorn, ed., *A Survey of the Contemporary Indians of Canada*, 2 vols. (Ottawa: Queen's Printer, 1966 and 1967).
31 Cairns, *Citizens Plus*, 161, 162n29.
32 Cairns, *Citizens Plus*, 163, 164. See also Harold Cardinal, *The Unjust Society: The Tragedy of Canada's Indians* (Edmonton: M.G. Hurtig, 1969).
33 Cairns, *Citizens Plus*, 164.
34 Cairns, *Citizens Plus*, 187.
35 Cairns, *Citizens Plus*, 187, 188.
36 Jessica Deer, "10 Indigenous candidates elected to House of Commons," *CBC News*, 22 October 2019, www.cbc.ca/news. See also Kathleen Martens, "Record-setting numbers of Indigenous candidates in 2019 race," 19 October 2019, www.aptnnews.ca.

37 J.R. Miller, *Residential Schools and Reconciliation: Canada Confronts Its History* (Toronto: University of Toronto Press, 2017), 243.

38 Miller, *Residential Schools and Reconciliation*, 243.

39 Miller, *Residential Schools and Reconciliation*, 247.

40 Miller, *Residential Schools and Reconciliation*, 247.

41 Miller, *Residential Schools and Reconciliation*, 248.

42 Miller, *Residential Schools and Reconciliation*, 271.

43 See, in particular, David Milward, "Freeing Inherent Aboriginal Rights from the Past," in *The Canadian Constitution in Transition*, edited by Richard Albert, Paul Daly, and Vanessa MacDonnell (Toronto: University of Toronto Press, 2019), 268. "Aboriginal-rights jurisprudence needs to enter a period of fundamental destabilization before it gets to a point where we can even think of rendering it more stable ... Professor Kaushal raises the valid point that enlarging the legal space for Aboriginal jurisdiction presents implications of profound destabilization for the constitutional federalist order. That, in my view, is also an acceptable implication of trying to improve the *situation of Aboriginal peoples*."

44 Gordon Christie, *Canadian Law and Indigenous Self-Determination: A Naturalist Analysis* (Toronto: University of Toronto Press, 2019).

45 Christie, *Canadian Law*, 3, 4.

46 Christie, *Canadian Law*, 403.

47 Christie, *Canadian Law*, 405.

48 Christie, *Canadian Law*, 408.

49 Christie, *Canadian Law*, 408.

50 Christie, *Canadian Law*, 411.

51 Aaron Mills, "Rooted Constitutionalism: Growing Political Community," in *Resurgence and Reconciliation: Indigenous–Settler Relations and Earth Teachings*, edited by Michael Asch, John Borrows, and James Tully (Toronto: University of Toronto Press, 2018), 133 at 160.

52 Mills, "Rooted Constitutionalism."

53 Mills, "Rooted Constitutionalism," 156.

54 Mills, "Rooted Constitutionalism," 157.

55 Mills, "Rooted Constitutionalism," 157.

56 Mills, "Rooted Constitutionalism," 158.

57 Aaron James Mills, *Miinigowiziwin: All That Has Been Given for Living Well Together: One Vision of Anishinaabe Constitutionalism* (PhD diss., University of Victoria, 2019), 274.

58 Mills, *Miinigowiziwin*, 159.

59 Glen Coulthard, *Red Skin, White Masks: Rejecting the Colonial Politics of Recognition* (Minneapolis: University of Minnesota Press, 2014).

60 Harsha Walia, "Land is a relationship": In conversation with Glen Coulthard on Indigenous nationhood," rabble.ca, 21 January 2015.
61 John Borrows, "Earth-Bound: Indigenous Resurgence and Environmental Reconciliation," in *Resurgence and Reconciliation*, ed. Asch, Borrows, and Tully, 49n50.
62 James Tully, "Reconciliation Here on Earth," in *Resurgence and Reconciliation*, ed. Asch, Borrows, and Tully, 83n50.
63 Tully, "Reconciliation," 117.
64 Tully, "Reconciliation," 113.
65 Tully, "Reconciliation," 115.
66 Tully, "Reconciliation," 117.
67 Tully, "Reconciliation," 83.
68 Tully, "Reconciliation," 83.
69 *Honouring the Truth, Reconciling for the Future: Summary of the Final Report of the Truth and Reconciliation Commission of Canada* (2015), 6.
70 Miller, *Residential Schools and Reconciliation*, 260n35.
71 *Canadian Public Opinion on Aboriginal Peoples: Final Report*, Environics Institute, 2016, www.environicsinstitute.org, 6.
72 Miller, *Residential Schools and Reconciliation*, 191n35.
73 A. Bagdonas, "Historical State Apologies," in *The Palgrave Handbook of State-Sponsored History after 1945*, 786, link.springer .com/chapter/10.
74 Truth and Reconciliation Commission of Canada, *Final Report*, vol. 6 (2015), 81.
75 Truth and Reconciliation Commission of Canada, *Final Report*, 81.
76 Kristy Kirkup, "Majority of Canadians find blockades of rail lines unacceptable: Poll," *Globe and Mail*, 9 March 2020, A7.
77 Kirkup, "Majority of Canadians," A7.
78 I offer my views on this subject in *University Commons Divided: Exploring Debate and Dissent on Campus* (Toronto: University of Toronto Press, 2018), 93–8.
79 Truth and Reconciliation Commission, "Call to Action," 43n70.
80 www.ctvnews.ca, 19 June 2019.
81 In 2018, Chief Na'Moks (John Ridsdale) told APTN News, "We've stripped the names from three female hereditary chiefs for supporting the pipeline." In Chris Selley, "This is no way to run a country," *National Post*, 13 March 2020, A8.
82 Selley, "This is no way."
83 In John Ivison, "A prize well worth pursuit: Structural reform urgently needed for First Nations," *National Post*, 22 February 2020, NP1.

84 John Graham, "Dysfunctional governance: Eleven barriers to progress among Canada's First Nations," inroadsjournal.ca. Graham is a governance consultant and former senior associate with the Institute on Governance. He has worked with Aboriginal communities for more than twenty-five years.

85 Graham, "Dysfunctional governance," 43.

86 Graham, "Dysfunctional governance," 43.

87 Greg Poelzer and Ken S. Coates, *From Treaty Peoples to Treaty Nation: A Road Map for All Canadians* (Vancouver: UBC Press, 2015), xxi.

4. Immigrants, Migration, and Citizenship

1 Readers will note that I have continued to use J.R. Miller's word "newcomers" to describe all non-Indigenous peoples who came to Canada, both in its early history and up to the present. There are some who use other words, including *settlers* and *colonizers*, often pejoratively, but those words do not accurately describe the 37 million Canadians of today and the diverse circumstances in which they were born in or came to Canada.

2 Statistics Canada definition, www150.statcan.gc.ca.

3 Oxford dictionaries.

4 Oxford dictionaries.

5 Mandate letter from Prime Minister Justin Trudeau to the Minister of Immigration, Refugees and Citizenship, 2019.

6 Momo Kano Podolsky and Monique Hutson, "Q&A with Joseph Carens: The Ethics of Immigration" (2015), munkschool.utoronto.ca.

7 Podolsky and Hutson, "Q&A with Joseph Carens."

8 Podolsky and Hutson, "Q&A with Joseph Carens."

9 Podolsky and Hutson, "Q&A with Joseph Carens."

10 Podolsky and Hutson, "Q&A with Joseph Carens."

11 Podolsky and Hutson, "Q&A with Joseph Carens."

12 See, for example, Harald Bauder, "It's time for Canada to truly open its borders," *Huffpost*, 6 December 2018.

13 Keith Neuman, "Canadian public opinion on immigration and refugees," Environics Institute, 2019, www.environicsinstitute.org.

14 Neuman, "Canadian public opinion."

15 Neuman, "Canadian public opinion."

16 Marc Montgomery, "Canadians' attitudes hardening against immigrants and refugees," Radio Canada International, 3 July 2019, www.rcinet.com.

17 Montgomery, "Canadians' attitudes hardening."

18 Montgomery, "Canadians' attitudes hardening."
19 Montgomery, "Canadians' attitudes hardening."
20 Montgomery, "Canadians' attitudes hardening."
21 Kaleigh Rogers, "Canadians' misperceptions about immigration reflect disinformation online," *CBC News*, 11 October 2019, www.cbc.ca.
22 Rogers, "Canadians' misperceptions."
23 Allison Harell, Stuart Soroka, and Shanto Iyengar, "Attitudes toward Immigration and Immigrants: The Impact of Economic and Cultural Cues in the U.S. and Canada," paper delivered at the APSA 2011 Annual Meeting, papers.ssrn.com.
24 Harell, Soroka, and Iyengar, "Attitudes," 16.
25 Harell, Soroka, and Iyengar, "Attitudes," 16.
26 Harell, Soroka, and Iyengar, "Attitudes," 16.
27 Harell, Soroka, and Iyengar, "Attitudes," 17.
28 These numbers are those of the United Nations Department of Economic and Social Affairs, www.un.org.
29 Tariq Khokhar and Haruna Kashiwase, "The Future of the World's Population in 4 Charts," *Data Blog*, 2015, blogs.world bank.org.
30 John Ibbitson and Darrell Bricker, *Empty Planet: The Shock of Global Population Decline* (Toronto: Penguin Random House, 2019).
31 Ibbitson and Bricker, *Empty Planet*, 20 February 2019, www.cbc.ca.
32 Ibbitson and Bricker, *Empty Planet*, www.amazon.ca.
33 See discussion in chapter 4.
34 Emma Groeneveld, "Early Human Migration," *Ancient History Encyclopedia*, 2017, www.ancient.eu.
35 Richard Breitman and Allan J. Lichtman, "The Real Story of the MS St. Louis," historynewsnetwork.org.
36 This story is told by Irving Abella and Harold Troper in None Is Too Many: Canada and the Jews of Europe, 1933–1948 (Toronto: University of Toronto Press, 1982).
37 Eli Yarhi, "MS St. Louis," *The Canadian Encyclopedia*, 2015, www .thecanadianencyclopedia.ca.
38 Maude-Emmanuelle Lambert, "Canadian Response to the 'Boat People' Refugee Crisis," *The Canadian Encyclopedia*, 2017, www .thecanadianencyclopedia.ca.
39 Lambert, "Canadian Response."
40 Lambert, "Canadian Response."
41 "This special report ... will argue, perhaps unpopularly, that the world needs more migration; that the potential gains vastly outweigh the costs,

and that those costs can be mitigated with better policies." "The magic of migration," Special Report, *The Economist*, 16 November 2019, 4.

42 "The magic of migration," *The Economist*.

43 "The magic of migration," *The Economist*, 3.

44 "The magic of migration," *The Economist*.

45 "The magic of migration," *The Economist*, 5.

46 "The magic of migration," *The Economist*, 6.

47 "The magic of migration," *The Economist*, 7.

48 "The magic of migration," *The Economist*, 6.

49 "The magic of migration," *The Economist*, 8.

50 "The magic of migration," *The Economist*, 9.

51 "The magic of migration," *The Economist*.

52 Niall Ferguson, "We let Lenin rise, millions died. Now it's Islamism" (2017), www.niallferguson.com.

53 David Frum, "Competing visions of Islam will shape Europe in the 21st century," *The Atlantic*, 2 May 2018, www.theatlantic.com.

54 Abdullahi Ahmed An-Na'Im, *Toward an Islamic Reformation* (Syracuse: Syracuse University Press, 1990), 184.

55 An-Na'Im, *Toward an Islamic Reformation*, book jacket.

56 In a previous book, I wrote: "What do we say of sentiments of some of Islamic faith that women should accept patriarchy and remain in their houses except when necessity compels them to go out? Or about an Imam in Montreal reported to have incited violence against Jews?" We should remind the former that their antediluvian views are contrary to the Charter, and the latter we should have prosecuted for hate speech." See Peter MacKinnon, *University Commons Divided: Exploring Debate and Dissent on Campus* (Toronto: University of Toronto Press, 2018), 117.

57 Pierre Desrochers and Joanna Szurmak, *Population Bombed! Exploding the Link between Overpopulation and Climate Change* (London: Global Warming Policy Foundation, 2018). This book was short-listed for the 2018 Donner Prize.

58 Desrochers and Szurmak, *Population Bombed!*, 57.

59 Desrochers and Szurmak, *Population Bombed!*, xix, xx.

60 Natalia Kanem, "Population and climate change," Climate 2020, 18 September 2017, www.climate2020.org.uk.

61 2020 Population Matters, populationmatters.org.

62 Eric Roston, "Earth needs fewer people to beat the climate crisis, scientists say," *Bloomberg Business News*, 5 November 2010, www .bloomberg.com.

63 Fiona Harvey, "Climate change soon to cause movement of 140 million people, World Bank warns," *The Guardian*, 19 March 2018, www .theguardian.com.
64 Cristina Cattaneo, "How does climate change affect migration," World Economic Forum, 23 November 2015, www.weforum.org.

5. Economic Opportunity and Citizenship

1 "V is for vicious," *The Economist*, 14 March 2020, 8.
2 Jordan Press, "Fact Check: How does Canada's growth stack up with the rest of the G7?," *The Canadian Press*, 6 February 2020, globalnews.ca.
3 OECD Better Life Index, www.oecdbetterlifeindex.org.
4 Craig Alexander, "Canada's competitiveness must be an election issue," *Globe and Mail*, 4 September 2019, www.theglobeandmail.com.
5 "What Canada's productivity challenge means for your business," www .business.hsbc.ca.
6 "Getting Down to Business: Investment and the Economic Outlook," remarks by Bank of Canada Deputy-Governor Lawrence Schembri to the Greater Vancouver Board of Trade, 21 March 2017, www.bankofcanafa.ca.
7 Philip Cross, "Business Investment in Canada Falls Far Behind Other Industrialized Countries," Fraser Institute: Fraser Research Bulletin, October 2017, www.fraserinstitute.org.
8 Neil Desai and Graeme Moffat, "Canada's innovation economy has been over-hyped and needs a reality check," *Globe and Mail*, 20 July 2018, www.theglobeandmail.com.
9 Leslie Preston, "U.S. leads in intellectual property products investment, while Canada lags," TD Economics, 17 October 2019, economics.td.com.
10 Conference Board of Canada Canadian Economic Forecast, March 2020.
11 Jeff Rubin, *The End of Growth* (Toronto: Random House Canada, 2012).
12 Richard Saillant, *A Tale of Two Countries: How the Great Demographic Imbalance Is Pulling Canada Apart* (Halifax: Nimbus, 2016).
13 Saillant, *A Tale of Two Countries*, 3.
14 Saillant, *A Tale of Two Countries*, 4.
15 Saillant, *A Tale of Two Countries*, 45.
16 Saillant, *A Tale of Two Countries*, 47.
17 He discusses innovation and new exploitation of natural resources and concludes that neither is on an existing or potential scale that it will alter the demographic. Saillant, *A Tale of Two Countries*, 48–55.
18 Saillant, *A Tale of Two Countries*, 154.

19 The Constitution Act of 1982, provides that "Parliament and the Government of Canada are committed to the principle of making equalization payments to ensure that provincial governments have sufficient revenues to provide reasonable comparable levels of public services and reasonably comparable levels of taxation."

20 Edison Roy-Cesar, "Canada's Equalization Formula," Atlas of Public Management, 2013, www.atlas101.ca.

21 Thomas J. Courchene, "A short history of equalization," *IRPP: Policy Options*, March 2007, policyoptions.irpp.org.

22 Daniel Beland, Andre Lecours, Gregory P. Marchildon, Haizhen Mou, and Rose Olfert, "The Challenge for Canada's Equalization Program," Public Policy Forum, 2018. policyoptions.irpp.org.

23 Beland et al., "The Challenge."

24 Beland et al., "The Challenge."

25 Beland et al., "The Challenge."

26 Beland et al., "The Challenge."

27 Steven Kirchner, "Lessons from the Australian Experience," in *Federalism and Fiscal Transfers*, edited by Jason Clemens and Niels Veldhuis (Vancouver: Fraser Institute, 2013), 23, 24, www.fraserinstitute.org.

28 Kirchner, "Lessons," 24.

29 Kirchner, "Lessons," 24.

30 Jason Clemens and Niels Veldhuis, *Federalism and Fiscal Transfers: Essays on Australia, Germany, Switzerland, and the United States* (Vancouver: Fraser Institute, 2013), www.fraserinstitute.org.

31 *Tear Down These Walls: Dismantling Canada's Internal Trade Barriers* (Ottawa: Standing Senate Committee on Banking, Trade and Commerce, 2016).

32 2018 SCC 15, [2018] 1 S.C.R. 342.

33 Trevor Tombe, "The good – and the bad – in Canada's provincial trade deal," *Maclean's*, 8 April 2017, www.macleans.ca.

34 Tombe, "The good."

35 Tombe, "The good."

36 Pete Evans, "3M faces pressure from Trump order to stop exporting N95 masks to Canada," *CBC News*, 3 April 2020, www.cbc.ca.

37 "Trucks, queues, and blues," *The Economist*, 28 March 2020, 63.

38 "Trucks, queues, and blues," *The Economist*, 63.

39 "Trucks, queues, and blues," *The Economist*, 64.

40 "Trucks, queues, and blues," *The Economist*, 64.

41 "Trucks, queues, and blues," *The Economist*, 64.

42 Bob Rae and Mel Cappe, "We can't just pick up the pieces after the pandemic subsides – we need to keep them together," *Globe and Mail*, 30 March 2020.

43 Philipp Carlsson-Szlezak, Martin Reeves, and Paul Swartz, "Understanding the Economic Shock of Coronavirus," BCG Centre for Macroeconomic Analysis, 27 March 2020, 1.

44 Carlsson-Szlezak et al., "Understanding the Economic Shock," 3, 4.

45 Carlsson-Szlezak et al., "Understanding the Economic Shock," 5.

46 Carlsson-Szlezak et al., "Understanding the Economic Shock," 8.

47 Carlsson-Szlezak et al., "Understanding the Economic Shock," 9.

6. Canadian Institutions and Citizenship

1 postmillennial.com, 9 March 2021.

2 Donald J. Savoie, *Democracy in Canada: The Disintegration of Our Institutions* (Montreal and Kingston: McGill–Queen's University Press, 2019). In the preface, Savoie describes the book as his magnum opus.

3 Savoie, *Democracy in Canada*, 368.

4 Savoie, *Democracy in Canada*, 368.

5 Savoie, *Democracy in Canada*, 17, 18.

6 Savoie, *Democracy in Canada*, 187.

7 Savoie, *Democracy in Canada*, 189.

8 Savoie, *Democracy in Canada*, 188.

9 Savoie, *Democracy in Canada*, 189. The observer was Lowell Murray, former minister in the government of Brian Mulroney.

10 Savoie, *Democracy in Canada*, x.

11 Savoie, *Democracy in Canada*, 237.

12 Savoie, *Democracy in Canada*, 237, 238.

13 Savoie, *Democracy in Canada*, 238.

14 Savoie, *Democracy in Canada*, 201.

15 Prime Minister Justin Trudeau changed the appointments process in favour of independent senators rather than partisans of alternating governing parties. It is too early to assess the full impact of the change or whether it will survive a change of government, but it does address the problem of partisan appointments, which in appearance and reality have undermined the Senate.

16 David E. Smith, *The Constitution in a Hall of Mirrors: Canada at 150* (Toronto: University of Toronto Press, 2017).

17 Smith, *The Constitution*, 135.

18 Smith, *The Constitution*, 142.
19 Smith, *The Constitution*, ix.
20 Smith, *The Constitution*, ix.
21 David Johnston, *Trust: Twenty Ways to Build a Better Country* (Toronto: Penguin Random House, 2018), ix.
22 "Majority of Canadians distrust government: Poll suggests," *CBC Radio*, 16 February 2017, www.cbc.ca.
23 Chrystia Freeland, "What happens when citizens lose faith in government?," *Reuters*, 5 August 2011, blogs.reuters.com.
24 Yuval Levin, "How did Americans lose faith in everything?," *New York Times*, 18 January 2020. www.nytimes.com
25 David Johnston, *Trust*, 4n20.
26 David Johnston, *Trust*, 4.
27 David Johnston, *Trust*, 4.
28 David Johnston, *Trust*, 4, 5.
29 David Johnston, *Trust*, 5.
30 "Canadians say they trust, get better value from their municipal governments than the feds or provinces," Ipsos Poll, July 2012, www .ipsos.com.
31 Savoie, *Democracy in Canada*, 264n1.
32 2020 Edelman Trust Barometer, www.edelman.com.
33 2020 Edelman Trust Barometer.
34 2020 Edelman Trust Barometer.
35 Alison Cretney and Juli Rohl, "The COVID-19 crisis has ushered in a 'Team Canada' spirit: Our energy industry needs the same," *Globe and Mail*, 21 May 2020, www.theglobeandmail.com.
36 Rutger Bregman, "The neoliberal era is ending: What comes next," *Correspondent*, 14 May 2020, https://the correspondent.com.
37 Abacus Data, Universities, Research and Canadian Public Opinion, 19 September 2017, abacusdata.ca.
38 George Fallis, *Multiversities, Ideas, and Democracy* (Toronto: University of Toronto Press, 2007), 343.
39 Fallis, *Multiversities*, 344.
40 Fallis, *Multiversities*, 346.
41 Fallis, *Multiversities*, 346.
42 Fallis, *Multiversities*, 350.
43 Fallis, *Multiversities*, 351.
44 Fallis, *Multiversities*, 352.
45 Peter MacKinnon, *University Commons Divided* (Toronto: University of Toronto Press, 2018).

46 Steven Levitsky and Daniel Ziblatt, *How Democracies Die* (New York: Penguin Random House, 2018).
47 Levitsky and Ziblatt, *How Democracies Die*, 3.
48 Levitsky and Ziblatt, *How Democracies Die*, 3.
49 Levitsky and Ziblatt, *How Democracies Die*, 3.
50 Levitsky and Ziblatt, *How Democracies Die*, 2.

7. What Is to Be Done?

1 Rex Murphy, "Get back or get out," *National Post*, 28 May 2020, A11. Murphy noted the House of Commons's oversight responsibility for the government's spending of $150 billion in response to the pandemic, one that cannot adequately be discharged when the House is not in session – in person or virtually.
2 David Crane, "We need a different kind of industrial strategy," *The Hill Times*, 1 June 2020.
3 Smith, *The Constitution* (see ch. 6, n. 16).
4 www.ipsos.com.
5 Andrew Potter, "Liberals and NDP have embraced contempt for Parliament," *National Post*, 30 May 2020, A4.
6 Anderson, *The Imperative of Integration* (see introduction, n. 1).
7 Lilla, *The Once and Future Liberal*, 119 (see ch. 1, n. 26).
8 Fukuyama, *Identity*, 183 (see ch. 1, n. 33).
9 Anderson, *The Imperative of Integration*.
10 Anderson, *The Imperative of Integration*, ch. 2.
11 Anderson, *The Imperative of Integration*, ch. 2.
12 Anderson, *The Imperative of Integration*, 183, 184.
13 Sharon Stanley, "*The Imperative of Integration*. By Elizabeth Anderson," *Journal of Politics* 74, no. 1 (2012): 1.
14 Stanley, "*The Imperative of Integration*," 1.
15 Potter, "Liberals and NDP."
16 Christian Joppke, "The Rise of Instrumental Citizenship," *Global Citizenship Review* (2018), globecit.com.
17 Joppke, "The Rise."
18 Transcript: Jennifer Welsh, "Where Do I Belong? Exploring Citizenship in the 21st Century," Hart House Lecture, 31 March 2004.
19 Welsh, "Where Do I Belong?"
20 Welsh, "Where Do I Belong?"
21 Kymlicka and Walker, *Rooted Cosmopolitanism*, "Introduction," n6.
22 Kymlicka and Walker, *Rooted Cosmopolitanism*, "Introduction," nn 20, 12.
23 Kymlicka and Walker, *Rooted Cosmopolitanism*, 13.

24 Kymlicka and Walker, *Rooted Cosmopolitanism*, 14.

25 Kymlicka and Walker, *Rooted Cosmopolitanism*, 14.

26 Kymlicka and Walker, *Rooted Cosmopolitanism*, 17.

27 Paul G. Thomas, "The Liberals promised to examine compulsory voting as part of electoral reform. But does Canada really need it?," *Policy Options*, 25 July 2016, policyoptions.irpp.org.

28 Thomas, "The Liberals promised."

29 Quoted in Tacey Rychter, "How compulsory voting Works: Australians explain," *New York Times*, 5 November 2018, www.nytimes.com.

30 Stephen Eric Bronner, "Interpreting the Enlightenment: Metaphysics, Critique, and Politics," *Logos* 3, no. 3 (Summer 2004): 17, www
.logosjournal.com.

31 Bruce Pardy, "Apocalyptic science: How the West is destroying itself," *Financial Post*, 26 June 2020.

32 The survey is discussed in Michael Adams, Max Finedaym and Keith Neuman, "The road to real reconciliation will be paved by Canada's youth," *Globe and Mail*, 4 August 2019, www.theglobeandmail.com.

33 Adams, Finedaym, and Neuman, "The road."

34 Adams, Finedaym, and Neuman, "The road."

35 See chapter 3, n80.

36 Frank Cassidy, "The First Nations Governance Act: A legacy of loss," *Policy Options*, 1 April 2003, policy options.irpp.org.

37 Don Drummond, "It is time for a Canadian Equitable Growth Institute," *Globe and Mail*, 15 February 2021.

38 Drummond, "It is time."

39 Drummond, "It is time."

40 Drummond, "It is time."

41 Drummond, "It is time."

42 I am among those concerned about the growing intolerance for pluralism and liberal democratic thought in our universities. I have written on the subject – see chapter 6, n44 – and have witnessed this intolerance in universities in which I have worked, including three in which I have served as president or interim president.

Afterword

1 "Have a happy Canada Day. Sorry," *Globe and Mail*, 1 July 2020, A12; and "I have found my place here: New Canadians reflect and offer advice for those just starting the journey," *Globe and Mail*, 1 July 2020, A1, A10, A11.

Index

 UTP insights

- Stephen M. Saideman, *Adapting in the Dust: Lessons Learned from Canada's War in Afghanistan*
- Michael R. Marrus, *Lessons of the Holocaust*
- Roland Paris and Taylor Owen (eds.), *The World Won't Wait: Why Canada Needs to Rethink Its International Policies*
- Bessma Momani, *Arab Dawn: Arab Youth and the Demographic Dividend They Will Bring*
- William Watson, *The Inequality Trap: Fighting Capitalism Instead of Poverty*
- Phil Ryan, *After the New Atheist Debate*
- Paul Evans, *Engaging China: Myth, Aspiration, and Strategy in Canadian Policy from Trudeau to Harper*